T0311159

The Art of the First Session

The Art of the First Session

MAKING PSYCHOTHERAPY COUNT
FROM THE START

ROBERT TAIBBI

W. W. Norton & Company
New York • London

For information about permission to reproduce selections from this book, write to Permissions, W. W. Norton & Company, Inc., 500 Fifth Avenue, New York, NY 10110

For information about special discounts for bulk purchases, please contact W. W. Norton Special Sales at specialsales@wwnorton.com or 800-233-4830

Manufacturing by RR Donnelley Westford
Production manager: Christine Critelli

Library of Congress Cataloging-in-Publication Data

ISBN 978-0-393-70843-1

W. W. Norton & Company, Inc.
500 Fifth Avenue, New York, N.Y. 10110
www.wwnorton.com

W. W. Norton & Company Ltd.
Castle House, 75/76 Wells Street, London W1T 3QT

1 2 3 4 5 6 7 8 9 0

To Susan

Contents

The Art of the First Session

INTRODUCTION

Making First Sessions Count

"So how did you get my name?"

Anne is dressed in business attire—this is her lunch hour, after all—and this is her first appointment with you. She actually has a pen in hand and a writing pad on her lap, at which she now quickly glances.

"Actually I found you online. It was one of the websites that lists all kinds of therapists by zip code. I read your profile and it said that you did cognitive-behavioral therapy [CBT]. I've read on the Mayo Clinic website about depression, and they cited research that showed that that approach is the most effective for treating depression. I've done that childhood exploration stuff a long time ago and I don't need more of that. And I looked at your profile and went to your website and it looks like you've had a lot of experience.

"I also did look at the profile of another therapist who looks like he specializes in CBT, but your office is closer to my work, and I think I might prefer to talk to a woman."

WELCOME TO 21ST-CENTURY THERAPY. Would you have had this type of conversation with a new client 10 years ago?

Maybe, but probably not. Twenty years ago? Definitely not. Back then there was no Internet on which to track down therapists. Anne may have gone to her family doctor, who would probably have given her a few names. If she had close friends and wasn't afraid of embarrassment, she might have pulled one of them aside in the break room and asked in hushed tones if he or she knew of any "good" therapists. She wouldn't have likely known about CBT and depression, and she probably would have just accepted whomever she got—preferring a woman, but if the guy seemed nice enough, she'd go with him. She didn't really have much of a choice.

The Landscape of Therapy

No more. According to some estimates, 70% of clients come from online searches (Therapytribe, 2014). Although some potential clients will still prefer to ask their doctors or friends, many are like Anne. They prefer the anonymity, the fact that the choices are likely to be many, that they can see pictures and read profiles. Just as patients now come to see their doctors waving articles on alternative treatments or the side effects of potential new medications that they've heard about on TV commercials, therapy clients are likely to be better informed than they were a decade ago. They can Google depression or AD/HD and see what the Mayo Clinic, NIH (National Institutes of Health), or WebMD recommends. As a result, the asymmetry of the relationship wherein the professional (doctor, therapist, even car salesperson) is in a one-up position with the client, holding and doling out all the information, is no longer present. The playing field is now a lot more level.

With that knowledge comes another big change in client expectations. Even if she hadn't been in therapy before, now having done her homework, watched YouTube videos, or picked up tidbits of what to expect from her sister who has been in therapy, Anne has a pretty clear idea of what she wants. And in a technological era of instant gratification, combined with insurance companies and mental health centers capping their sessions to reduce costs or waiting lists, most clients are expecting to skip your three-session assessment model and are ready to hit the ground running.

All this seems so different from those *New Yorker* cartoons of patients plopped down on the analyst's couch, offering lingering images of what we think therapy used to be. But the reality is that it hasn't been that way for a long time. Past and present research tells us that most clients haven't and don't stick around too long. Whereas the average client comes to therapy five to eight times (Cooper, 2011), most come only once (Phillips, 1985), and 70% drop out before reaching their goals (Garfield, 1986).

So what does this all mean? Several things. Clients today are better informed and can generally afford to be discerning and even fussy about the therapist with whom they work. They can shop around online, do a brief meet-and-greet, and are likely to interview you as much as you interview them. Clients expect results and likely won't stick around if they don't get them. They are looking, not unlike those shopping for a new computer or automobile, for the Right Product—a clinical approach that can fix their problems—and the Right Person—the person who can deliver in terms of skill as well as plain old likeability and trust.

After the client has plowed through the profiles and the websites and finally made it to your office—and if it's true that you only have one chance to make a good impression—that chance is here in that first session. This is where the mix of expectations and presentation, of matching what the client wants with what you have to offer, all come together. This is the time and place where you need to be "on your game," merging your clinical skills with your personal style; here is when clients absolutely need to feel differently when they walk out than when they walked in.

Selling Therapy

You may not think of yourself as a salesperson, but like it or not, you are. Daniel Pink, the author of *To Sell Is Human* (2013), commissioned a large nationwide study and found that Americans are spending 40% of work time in what he calls *nonsales selling*. Although you may not be hawking a used car, computer, or refrigerator, a significant portion of your work is persuading people to "buy" your idea—that their depression arises from how they think, that their child isn't just a "bad kid" but has a clinical diagnosis known as attention-deficit disorder, that your focus on the past or the present or the family dynamics is effective in treating their anxiety, anger, eating disorder, or addiction. Just as your silence in therapy is always more than just silence, whatever you do or say with clients always includes, at some level, selling.

And though this notion of selling may initially seem like an uncomfortable way of thinking about your work, realize that persuading and influencing are actually not new, but rather things you've likely been doing your whole life. Even as a child you were probably working the babysitter to let you stay up later; as a teenager you were likely trying to sell your parents on the idea of letting you go to beach week or stay out past your curfew on a Saturday night. So even if you don't look like that used-car salesman with the plaid suit and slicked-back hair, just like him, you're making your therapy pitch to folks like Anne, just as Anne, from her side of the room, is considering whether or not to take you and your approach for a test drive.

What is different is that your aim is not to manipulate the client to satisfy your own ends, but rather to take what you know about human psychology and emotional distress to ensure that this particular client understands how you think and what you can offer. And although clients may be more in the driver's seat than they used to be, and although there's pressure on you to sell yourself as the Right Product and the Right Person, this doesn't mean you need to compromise your clinical approach and style. It requires only that you be more deliberate and acutely aware of what is happening and needs to happen in the first hour. You do your best, and then it's up to Anne to decide whether this is a good fit.

The Art of the First Session: An Overview

Unlike other texts on first sessions that detail the content of the session—what you need to cover in terms of mental status exams, assessing children or families, questions to ask, developing diagnoses—our focus will be different. We'll be talking instead about process—how to shape and guide this critical first session—and presenting a roadmap—defining essential elements, dos and don'ts, even offering mini-scripts of what you can say to address certain issues—so you can hit the ground running. Our approach will be generic so that you can apply these skills and way of thinking to whatever your core theoretical approach may be.

We're also going to build into our model some of the knowledge from the world of sales concerning what works and doesn't in terms of influencing and persuading those sitting across from you. Actually the sales profession has gone through its own revolution, and is now much more like therapy than therapy was ever like sales. Gone are the days of the hard-sell, the Always-Be-Closing mantra of *Glengarry Glen Ross*. Twenty years ago only 10% of a sales meeting focused on building trust, now it is 40%; then 20% of the time was spent on "qualifying the client" (essentially making sure they could afford what you were selling), whereas now 30% of the time is spent on "listening to their needs"; the sales presentation was 30% of your time, now it is 20%; and finally, your closing was 40% of what you did, now it's a mere 10% (Tracy, 2008).

The shift is dramatic: 70% of the selling is now building the relationship—very therapy-like, yes? The belief is that you take the time to lay down this solid foundation of trust, listen actively and closely to find out what the client is seeking most; what you present and how you wrap it up becomes secondary because it will all fall into place if you do the first part right. Clients will realize on their own, without your arm-twisting, that this is the Right Product and that you are the Right Person. We'll use some of this road-tested knowledge to help you make the most of the that first session: to build that foundation of trust, determine client expectations and needs, gather the information you need to make an assessment, and create and present a preliminary treatment plan that enables you to "close the deal."

We'll start off in the first chapter by defining the critical first-session skills that you need most: tracking the process, changing the emotional climate, anticipating transference issues, preparing ahead for the session, and controlling the clock. *Tracking the process*—the ability to stay in lockstep with the client all through the session—is an essential skill and particularly one that less experienced clinicians can easily lose sight of. Like the clients themselves, new clinicians can get mired in the swamp of content. *Changing the emotional climate* means that clients need to feel differently when they walk out than when they walk in, and there are techniques you can use and opportunities you need to look for to make sure this happens. *Preparation* refers not only to effectively presenting yourself before you ever meet the client, but also having on deck a game plan made up of hypotheses and treatment maps so that you are not reinventing the wheel with each client but instead are able to feel and convey confidence. *Controlling the clock* is the reality checker of the first session, and like the football coach, you always want to make sure you still have time for that last big play.

In Chapters 2 and 3 we will break down the structure and process of the first session: Chapter 2 focuses on the seven goals that you need to accomplish, as well as the clinical potholes you want to avoid; in Chapter 3 we'll actually walk through the first session, start to finish, focusing on the opening and setting the foundation, the middle with its exploration and changing of the emotional climate, and the closing when you redefine the problem, offer a plan, and close the deal.

If Chapter 3 provides the template for a solid first session, Chapter 4 covers those situations when everything goes less than ideally: the openly resistant client, the emotional client, the ambivalent or inhibited client. The process is the same; what changes is your focus and your guiding of the process.

These first four chapters center primarily on individuals as a first-session model. In Chapter 5 we consider couples and how working with them differs—the need to maintain balance, avoid playing courtroom, help them define process rather than only focusing on content—essential skills for working with this often-difficult population. In Chapter 6 we do the same with families and talk about integrating young children and teens into the process and how to manage the interactions of multiple clients at one time.

Finally in Chapter 7 we'll move to life beyond the first session to consider ways of keeping the momentum going, anticipating the challenges, and integrating first-session skills and concepts into your own clinical style. Along the way there will be plenty of composited case examples and vignettes to help you hit the ground running.

Let's get started.

CHAPTER 1

Critical First-Session Skills

To be a bit dramatic for a moment, the first session isn't just a session, it's a state of mind. It's different from other therapy sessions because it is a beginning. And like any new beginning—your first overnight, your first kiss, your first big trip by yourself without parents, the first day on your first big job, the birth of your first child—it has its own character and impact. Unlike those next therapy sessions ("So, how was your week?"), routine has not yet taken hold in the first session. Regardless of your experience, there's always anticipation, being a bit on edge, not exactly sure what is going to unfold. There's always some angst about whether this will work clinically, in terms of matching your approach to client needs and personally, whether the client and you both feel like it is a good fit.

This state of mind is about you. You now are the captain of the ship welcoming the newcomer on board. You are the one who feels the pressure to present what you do and how you do it in the best possible light, to guide the process so that what needs to get done here gets done well. This is not a time to lapse into autopilot, to engage the same familiar process that you can easily do most days, hour by hour. This is a special occasion. A big performance. The first drive of the game.

And it is a first for the client as well. On the other side of the room is someone who has spent considerable emotional and mental effort to make it to your office and see what you have to offer. The person has sloughed through endless websites about therapy and therapists to get to yours with high hopes and expectations, has taken time off from work, rearranged her schedule a week ago or more, nailed down babysitters, and obsessed over what to say to you and what you're going to say in response.

In this chapter we'll cut through all that performance pressure by mapping out the primary skills you need to successfully move through this exciting beginning process.

Skill Set #1: Tracking the Process

Michael arrives for his first session and his first experience of therapy. He immediately starts talking about last Saturday night. He and his girlfriend had an argument, but it wasn't like other arguments they'd had before. This one escalated quickly, and Michael finally got so frustrated and angry that he pushed his girlfriend against the wall. She screamed at him to get out, which he did. She won't talk to him, and he feels guilty and shaken. But he realizes that although this is the first time he was physically assaultive with his girlfriend, he has had times even at work where he snaps at a coworker when the person doesn't follow through and meet a deadline. And his father had the same problem, he used to. . . .

It's great that Michael is so open, but you can't afford to have Michael go on and on like this for the entire session while you just listen. Why? Because although he might feel better because he got a lot off his chest, when you call a halt to the session he may also feel that he didn't really get much in return from you for his time and money. And even if he doesn't mind that, being new to therapy, he may leave with the mistaken impression that this is what therapy is all about, which may not be your style of therapy at all.

There's also a danger here that you will get lost in a *War and Peace* novel, buried in this heap of information, stuck in the weeds of too many characters, too many incidents, too much backstory. This scenario makes for the notorious progress notes of less experienced therapists—pages and pages of facts, events, and situations with no clear path through them. Finally, you have a lot of things to get done in this first session besides hearing the story of Michael's life, and if you just sit there and let him run, there's a good chance you're just going to plain run out of time.

You and the client in this first session are essentially speaking two different languages. Michael, like most clients (especially those new to therapy), is speaking the language of content: the facts, the story, the information. This is how his mind works. Who said what, when, what happened next, his parents, the history of their relationship, etc. He instinctively believes that if he gives you more and more information, you will understand him and his problem better. He will make his case, you will sort it all out, decide what elements are right or wrong, whether he is connecting the dots in the right way, and tell him what he needs to fix.

You care about what he has to offer, but only to a certain point. Your language and your leadership focuses on *process*: on seeing how the relationship in the room between you and the client unfolds, what nonverbal reactions combine with what emotions. The way he is with you may somehow mirror what he is like when he is dealing with his girlfriend or coworker. You want to know about his content, but in the context of the session process. This is 70% of your focus, and when you get stuck, this is what you always return to. Process is your domain and you are the one in charge of shaping it.

So this becomes the first skill set: to *track and shape the session process*. The practical reason is to control the clock, which we'll talk about in a few moments. The other is to accomplish the goals that are essential to a successful first session: rapport building, assessing, changing the emotional climate, making your pitch, and presenting your treatment plan. But one of the primary reasons for tracking the process is to ensure that you and the client stay in lockstep throughout. First, a personal story:

When I was in college I worked for several weeks selling encyclopedias door to door (remember books?). I only did this for several weeks because it was awful. I was dropped off in strange neighborhoods in the middle of winter at night, left to bang on doors, hoping someone would let me in and let me stay long enough to do my pitch. There was actually training (about 20 minutes) about the process of making the pitch, should the salesperson ever get past the front door.

Essentially, the training consisted of instructions to move from selling point to selling point. For example, I might say: "So, by having an encyclopedia in your home, your children have ready access to any information they need, and you don't have to worry about dragging them to the library late at night or on Saturday [remember, pre-Internet]. And you don't have to worry that the encyclopedia will become dated because every year there is an annual book that you can purchase for a nominal fee that will supply all the new information. . . ."

I was told to look for agreement after making each selling

point—the nod of the head, a smile, and positive word. This is the concept of *getting yeses all the way down the line*. If I was able to get those yeses, then when it came time to close the deal—to talk about money and sign on the dotted line— customers would, more than likely, do so. The rub came if I missed something. If the parents frowned, for example, when I mentioned the annual book cost, or if I didn't answer their objection about the price to their satisfaction, when it came time to close, they would balk.

Think about your last major purchase, for example, a new car, a stove, a washing machine. The salesperson first narrowed down what you were looking for, and then started to educate you about the features: "So this particular vehicle comes with an overdrive system built into the engine. It cost $800 more, but it delivers 20% better fuel efficiency." Or, "This stove has in addition to a regular oven, a convection feature as well. Although it costs $200 more, it actually browns food evenly and shortens cooking time by 25%, saving you in electricity costs." A good salesperson would then wait to hear what you said next: "I can't afford the $800" or "I don't really use the oven that much, so the convection feature doesn't matter to me."

What the salesperson is doing is trying to stay in lockstep with you, narrowing down what it is you want, need, or agree with, and what you don't, and not letting any objections go by without addressing them. You, the therapist, need to do essentially the same thing: track the process, stay in lockstep with the client, narrow down and define his or her expectations and needs, and address expectations as they arise.

What do these points mean in terms of shaping the therapeutic process? Let's look at some examples:

Monitor Verbal Agreement and Objections

It seems obvious to monitor agreements and objections, but it's easy to let objections go by in the press of time or to miss the subtle versions. If you say to your client, "So I suggest that we start out by meeting twice a week," you wait and see what she says next. "That's great!" she says enthusiastically. Good to go. If instead she says, "I was thinking of only coming once a week," you now have a problem in the room that needs to be addressed. "Tell me why twice a week may be a problem?" you say. The client says that she can't take that much time off from her job, or that she can't afford paying for two sessions. You now address those issues: "Can you come after work?"; "Do we need to make some adjustments in the fee?"; or "Let me explain why I think the two sessions may be more effective."

The trickier client response is, "Sure, that's sounds fine, I guess." Hmmm. You hear the hesitation, the caution, but you don't ignore it. This becomes the new problem that you need to address: "You sound hesitant. I'm wondering why. Is there a problem with coming twice a week?"

Monitor Nonverbal Cues

As a therapist you're no doubt automatically sensitive to nonverbal communication, but it's easy, if you're mentally caught up splicing together elements of the client's story, to miss some important cue. You say, "Twice a week," and the client says fine, but then looks away. You don't want to let this go by: "You sound like twice a week is okay, but you look uncertain. I'm wondering if you have some hesitations about coming that often." On the other side, you want to pay attention to agreement—the nodding of the head, the eye contact, the smile. These let you know that you are walking in lockstep on the path.

Pay Particular Attention to Interpretations

So after Michael's lengthy description of his father and their relationship, you might say, "I'm thinking that you may have understandably identified with your father when you were growing up." You now see what he says next: "Oh my God, I never thought of that, that makes absolute sense!" Or, "I'm nothing like my father, I don't think so!" Or, " Sure, I guess, maybe I did."

Interpretations are often critical interventions in a number of therapeutic approaches with the aim of bringing the client into some important awareness and realization. When they are solidly endorsed by the client—"Oh my God, my father!"—they open up not only a new perspective on the self, but also a new path of exploration in the therapy. But if the client openly rejects your interpretation—"My father! That makes no sense to me!"—your next step is clear: to find out how Michael thinks about it differently, perhaps by saying, "It sounds like you think about it differently; tell me how." What you don't want to do is essentially bypass the emotional reaction in the room and fall into a mini-power struggle, stacking up more and more evidence to press your point: "I'm saying this because you may not realize that. . . . "

The greater challenge comes in the middle ground— "Sure, I guess"— the yes-but response whereby the client is verbally agreeing while giving nonverbal cues indicating that he or she is not fully on board with the idea. If you accept the verbal and push aside the nonverbal message—the ambivalent tone—you'll be wondering several sessions down the road why Michael doesn't seem to be as engaged as he used to be or is calling in sick with a cold.

The point here is that you need to track the process like a bloodhound. Nose to the ground of session interaction, alert to places where the client has drifted off in a different direction or has hung back and is not moving with you. With individuals this is relatively easy to do if you make process your focus and avoid getting stuck in decoding all the facts and stories that the client is presenting. With couples and families, following the trails of the individual clients can be more difficult: The father nods his head while the mother shakes hers. If you pick only one—your temptation might be to follow the father (follow the agreement)—you risk losing the spouse. You need to pay attention to both, again by keeping your nose to ground.

Skill Set #2: Changing the Emotional Climate

Changing the emotional climate is, in many ways, cousin to tracking the process in that the two go hand in hand. *Changing the emotional climate* means that clients need to feel differently when they walk out than when they walked in. If they don't, they probably won't come back. Facilitating this change can be done on a cognitive level, by helping them think differently about their problem, which in turn, changes how they feel, by tapping into new emotions so that they actually are feeling differently, or a combination of both.

No doubt you often do this instinctively throughout the course of therapy. The reason we're breaking this out so explicitly as a separate skill set is to underscore its importance in the first session. You need to deliberately look for opportunities to create this shift as the session unfolds. If done sensitively, by closely tracking the process to be certain the client is not feeling overwhelmed, the client will leave feeling that indeed something new came out of the session; he or she will attribute it, rightfully, to your skill.

So, how to create this climate change? By "going where clients are *not* going"—by focusing on what they are not presenting in the room, in order to help them step outside their emotional comfort zones. Here are some of the common techniques.

Focus on Soft or Opposite Emotions

Frank admits that he is an easily angered guy. Right now he's ranting about the way his supervisor is always singling him out for criticism. What Frank doesn't express are any softer emotions—sadness, fear, worry—and so this is where you go: "Frank, you sound angry. But what are you most worried about? What are you afraid will happen if your supervisor keeps treating you like this?" If you voice your question in a soft tone, the language of worry and fear will help Frank tap into these underlying, less comfortable emotions. The emotional climate in the room will change.

You can also create these shifts by picking up on the nonverbal cues: for example, noticing how Maria is tearing up as she rationally explains what happened the night before. You move away from content and focus on the emotion: "Maria, hold on for a moment. You're looking sad. What is going on inside you?" At this point, if you say this quietly, gently, so she can relax her defenses, as Frank did, Maria may begin to cry.

This is good, but at some point in the first session you'll want to try and move her toward those opposite, stronger emotions: "What do you do when you get angry?" "Do you ever get fed up or feel that it's not fair?" "Are there times when you realize that it isn't your fault and feel calm?" Rather than letting her leave the session replicating the emotions she already knows—sad and victimized—you want to help her tune into her power and emotional strength.

Make Language More Detailed

Alan says he is struggling with "grief"; Anna says that she and her husband had a "terrible fight" on Saturday night; Emily says she gives herself a "hard time."

"What do you mean," you say to Alan, "when you say you are 'struggling with grief?' What are you feeling, what do you think about?"

"Can you describe for me what exactly happened on Saturday night?" you ask Anna. "What were you arguing about? Who started it?"

"What happens when you give yourself a 'hard time'?" you say to Emily. "What do you say to yourself? What triggers your doing this?"

You're not drilling down into content here, you're drilling down into emotions. Emotions are connected to language. Vague, general comments lead to vague, general emotions. Using more detailed language—helping clients say more about what they are feeling, marching with them, step by step, through their arguments—evokes more succinct emotions into which you then can tap.

Ask Hard Questions

"Have you ever considered divorce? If you didn't have children, would you stay?" "Have you ever thought of suicide?" "Are you worried that you will never find a good job?" Asking hard questions requires you to say aloud what you think the client may have thought at some point. Not only does it let clients know that you can handle such deeper and tougher conversations, it also shifts the mood to a deeper level—from describing their problems, for example, to homing in on their bottom lines.

Reframe Problems as Bad Solutions to Other Problems

One way of looking at any presenting problem is that it is a bad solution to another problem beneath it. Procrastination isn't a problem, but a bad solution to some anxiety. Drinking isn't a problem but a bad solution to depression or anger. Affairs aren't a problem but a bad solution to a frozen relationship, poor self-esteem, or years of feeling like a martyr.

You don't need to figure out for what the problem is a solution. This is a specific type of hard question, and you merely need to ask it: "If your [restate client's presenting problem] is a bad solution to another problem beneath it, what do you think that problem might be?" And then see what happens next. Again the climate in the room is likely to change. The conversation can now shift from emotions tied to the presenting problem to emotions that cluster around the deeper issue.

Give Voice to an Ideal Scenario

Antonio is describing how his father has always been critical of him, that he is resentful that even now as an adult, his father is never supportive, is always giving advice that he never asks for. Often their phone conversations end with Antonio getting frustrated and hanging up. They then both don't talk for a while, the father will eventually call, they will say nothing about the last phone call, and the pattern will start over again.

"What would happen," you say, "if you called up your father or sent him an email and said something like this: 'Dad, I know you always want to the best for me, and you have worked hard all your life to give me what you never had, and I appreciate that. But sometimes when I'm trying to tell you about things that are important to me or things that I am struggling with, you jump in and sound critical, probably because you get worried, and you start offering advice rather than listening. I'm not trying to be critical, but my feelings get hurt and most of all it gets in the way of our being closer.' What do you think your father would say if you said that to him?" You may not know exactly what Antonio will say next, but if you voice this ideal scenario in a gentle manner, it is likely that his mood will shift and soften.

Think of this technique as a mini role play where you are giving voice to what the client or the other may be thinking but not saying, that taps into the softer emotions (appreciation, hurt, worry) that are often overshadowed by the stronger emotions of anger, frustration, or resentment. In this case you are expressing Antonio's hurt feelings and his desire to be heard, as well as the father's benevolent intentions that might lie under what Antonio sees as criticism or control. You are providing the subtext, the deeper and more complete emotions and thoughts that clients and those they are in relationships with struggle to fully say; as the client describes the relationship dynamics, imagine how they would unfold ideally, if they could.

And even if Antonio's first reaction is to push aside what you just said—"My father would probably just deny he does that"—you are moving the conversation in the room in a new direction, toward exploring what might make the father mentally tick. These articulations and enactments can be emotionally powerful, both changing the climate in the room and modeling for the client a new way of interacting.

Provide Education

Education, that is, giving information to clients about problems and psychological processes, can work on several levels to change the emotional climate. What you say will obviously depend upon your theoretical foundation—psychodynamic, narrative, cognitive-behavioral, systems, and so on—but the effects are still the same. Education reframes the problem, placing it a new context, allowing the client to think about it in a new way.

When you say to a mother, for example, that it sounds like her teenage son isn't necessarily a "moody bad kid" but instead is showing symptoms of bipolar disorder and explain its characteristics and treatment, the mother has a different lens through which to view him and his behavior. Similarly, when you say that what seems like control is often driven by an underlying and steady state of anxiety, or that given the child's abuse history it makes sense that she is fearful of separation and not something she should feel responsible for, the client has a new story to replace the old. This is what your family doctor does when he or she says that the skin rash isn't the rare disease you thought it might be, but instead a normal physical reaction to an allergen. You, as the worried patient, feel more relaxed.

And with education comes normalization. When you say to the spouses who have been married 6 years that there really is a 7-year itch where the initial psychological contract between the partners has changed because their needs have naturally changed over time, the message is that what they are experiencing is not abnormal at all. It's no longer that "I'm screwed up" or "You're screwed up," but rather that "We're going through a common evolution of our relationship with which most people struggle." Similarly, when you say to the young mother that some children are born with slow-to-warm temperaments that cause them to be naturally cautious, she no longer worries that her child will stand out as unusual or that there is something deeply wrong with her.

This process of normalization is closely related to the notion of consensus that is one of the key elements in successful sales. Here the salesperson mentions to a potential buyer what other customers have thought or done—for example, "Most customers tend to like the side-by-side doors on this refrigerator; it makes it easier to see what is in the freezer than does a bottom draw model." Not only do we feel better knowing that others have the same questions, reactions, and experiences, we're also apt to rely on such consensus if we are undecided. What works in sales also works in first sessions.

Education can also be a strong counter to heavy emotion. The client who feels overwhelmed, self-critical, or deeply depressed not only gains a new perspective through the information you provide, but also through the process of education itself you are helping the client move out of the emotional state of mind into a more rational one. Again, think family doctor. With her diagnosis comes a calm explanation of the biological process or the effects the medication has, or what research has shown to be the long-term results. The tone in the room changes. Not only does such talk underscore your own impressions of the doctor's knowledge and skill, and hence build trust, but her presentation and language help pull you out of your anxious emotional mind.

Finally, when you incorporate education into your pitch toward the end of the session, it can have the effect of bringing together all that has been discussed, explored, and expressed throughout the session into a clear focus. We'll talk more about this process in Chapter 3.

Once again, the point of all these techniques is to deliberately create a change in the client's state of mind by the end of the session. Your challenge is to look for opportunities throughout the session to include these techniques in the session process, and then to closely track the client's reactions to see what impact they have. Should things go off course—your educational pitch is misunderstood, your ideal scenario technique creates further distress, your move toward softer emotions only confuses the client—back up. Explain where you are going, why you are asking such questions or making such statements, and link them to the client's motivation, namely the presenting problems. For example: "I'm asking you to tell me more about the argument because you said that you didn't understand how things got out of control so quickly"; "I'm asking you about your childhood not to dredge up the past but because you said that you always feel like you are on edge; sometimes children learn to cope in this way if they grow up in chaotic or highly emotional families." And then see what happens next, adjust again, and move forward.

Skill Set #3: Anticipating Transference Issues

If you've ever gone shopping for a car, the car salesperson might have asked you what other cars you may have already considered. If you go see your physician for depression, he may ask if you have ever been on an antidepressant before and whether it helped. What both the salesperson and doctor are trying to find out is what to do and, more importantly, what *not* to do. If you mention that you looked at the equivalent-sized Ford but thought it was too expensive for what you would get, the salesperson will know to talk about price and point out the many features that are standard. Similarly, when you say to the doctor that you tried Prozac in the past but quit after a month because you didn't like the sexual side effects, he knows to steer you away from Prozac and toward a different medication with fewer sexual side effects.

All this makes sense; it's part of narrowing down what a client needs and wants so that the product matches the person. You can do the same when you ask clients at the beginning of the session if they have been in therapy before and what their experience was:

"Yes, I saw another therapist briefly a few months ago."

"And why didn't you go back and see her again?"

"Well, I felt she was nice, but all she did was listen and didn't give me any feedback or advice."

Note to self: Don't just listen, but also provide feedback and advice.

There is still a deeper level to such exploration beyond clarifying expectations, and that is anticipating transference issues. Just as you use the ideal scenario to present a more complete and complex perspective on a problem or relationship, you want to present yourself in the first session as, for lack of a better term, an ideal parent. This does not require that you spend an excessive amount of time exploring the past, but rather that you listen carefully to the ways clients describe various relationships in their current lives. This is attending to the subtleties of building the therapeutic relationship; if you do it well, it too will change the session climate.

If Tamara complains, for example, that her boyfriend is always critical, or Sam says that his boss is unappreciative of all that he does, or Heather mentions that her mother was always cold and distant, you immediately know what *not* to do. Out of all that these clients could talk about in their relationships, they are focusing on specific aspects: Tamara on criticism, Sam on lack of appreciation, Heather on coldness and distance. That they are sensitive to these feelings and dynamics rather than others usually indicates some underlying childhood wound. If you can listen for such comments, you'll know what you need to do to avoid retriggering and rewounding the client. If you miss this clue and inadvertently step upon clients' old wounds, they are likely not to return.

So you want to deliberately be complimentary and supportive of Tamara; appreciative of Sam's past efforts; and be empathic, warm, and even a bit self-disclosing (perhaps) with Heather. And if you inadvertently trigger these old wounds— you ask Tamara why she didn't do <fill in the blank>, and she reacts defensively or makes a face—you immediately neutralize the reaction by explaining in a gentle voice that you are not being critical but rather just trying to understand better how she thinks through certain situations. Ditto for Sam and Heather if they have reactions that are more negative than you would expect.

Once you recognize a client's transference reactions, you always want to assume that it takes little to trigger them. Your furrowed brow goes unnoticed by most clients, but Tamara notices and suspects disapproval, and so you explain clearly what you are thinking in the moment to counteract any assumption she may make. Your being tired and having low energy is no problem for most, but you know that Heather could interpret it as a withdrawal, and so you mention that you didn't sleep well and apologize if you seem a bit more sluggish than you were the week before. When you compliment Sam on how well he completed his homework assignment, you make certain that the compliment emotionally registers with him. You stay alert to these potential distortions; you heighten your response—sound more gentle, be more supportive and appreciative—with these clients than you may usually do with others. It's not about being manipulative, not about giving up your own style and approach, but simply being sensitive and aware so that old wounds don't derail the treatment process and relationship.

Although many seasoned therapists seem to be able to uncover and manage transferences instinctively, there is a skill set in place from which the rest of us can learn. The starting point is attuning to these early clues in clients' stories. You want to be careful not to miss the clues by getting too caught up in the story itself or to hear them as only background information that you may or may not return to—for example, a few sessions later when you do a more formal social history with Heather—and disregard them at the beginning. The challenge is to put this transference information into play right away. If you do, clients may not automatically think that you're supportive, appreciative, or warm, but more likely that that you're likeable, nice, easy to talk to. What is most important is that they don't leave feeling those familiar negative feelings they've come to associate with those with whom they struggle.

Skill Set # 4: Preparing Ahead

Tracking the process, actively seeking ways to change the emotional climate, and anticipating transference issues do much of the heavy lifting during the first session; they are the foundation that shapes the overall process. To use a track analogy, they are the core skills for running the race. Preparing ahead is the important warm-up that allows you to hit the ground running. There are actually two elements to this preparation: what you actually *do* before the session, and what you *think about* before the session (the development of treatment maps). We'll take them one by one.

Initial Contacts

As mentioned in the introduction, most clients have already done a lot of work to get to your office before you even meet. They've looked online at therapist directories or gotten your name from a friend or doctor and Googled you, checked out your website, compared and contrasted you and what you offer against other therapists in your area. Some impression is likely already in place, and with it some setting of expectations.

Precontact Contacts. Just as you are going to be deliberate and proactive in the first session, you are going to prepare the same way before the session. If you've read anything about marketing and branding yourself in our technological age, you know how important these are. If you belong to an online therapist referral site that includes your profile, or if you have your own website (and you should), you need to be sensitive to and critical of what you post—this is, after all, a potential client's first impression of you. You need to have the right photo where you look both relaxed and professional (not the blurry one your husband took at the beach where you look at bit dazed), have the right statement letting potential clients quickly and clearly know your strengths (20 years experience), your style (interactive, cognitive-behavioral approach), and your primary areas of specialty (children, depression, trauma).

Because potential clients are usually online seeking professionals who work with their particular problem, as opposed to searching for a particular therapist (perhaps you), it's good to avoid vague statements ("helping you create more caring relationships," "helping you be who you most want to be") that say little about what you can specifically offer and do. Decide what is the one impression that you want readers to walk away with after visiting your site: what it is that you do best, what defines your clinical style, what will help you *stand out* from the rest.

Similarly, your voicemail message should be professional and authoritative sounding—no mumbling, no rambling, no background noises that sound like you are recording it in the middle of a truck stop or that your kids are in the room doing a drum concert on the kitchen pots and pans.

If potential clients reach out to you via email or phone, or even text, assume they are in crisis because most are, in some way. You should also assume that they are probably reaching out to other clinicians as well. What this means is that you need to respond quickly. (Think how quickly the car salesperson spots you on the lot.) Clients not only feel frustrated when you take long to respond (or never do), but it also soils their impression and potentially your reputation.

If they send an email, respond to clients' questions. Usually these are about whether you have openings, take their insurance, have weekend appointments, and so forth. In your reply you can also refer them to your website and encourage them to call or write back if they need to know more. If you are responding to a voicemail message and know that you don't really have enough time (10 minutes is an ample amount of time to allocate) to talk with a potential client till several hours later, it's often a good idea to call and leave a message saying precisely that: "Hi, Carol. I just want to let you know that I did get your message a little while ago, and I'm going to be tied up until 4:00 this afternoon. I will give you a call then, and if that time doesn't work, let me know if another time does and I'll give you call." Potential clients like knowing that you received the message, and they appreciate your efforts to be responsive.

Initial Phone Call. And when you get Carol, in person, on the phone, don't rush. Ask if she has any specific questions for you. Ask what she needs help with the most and give her a three-sentence summary of your approach and style to gauge whether you can deliver the Right Product and be the Right Person. That said, don't turn this into a phone first session. Although it's possible to do therapy via phone, you don't want to use that mode for a first session, in which building rapport is based on nonverbal behaviors; it's simply best to see the person face-to-face. If Carol is in crisis, try to schedule a session with her as quickly as possible, rather than spending 45 minutes on the phone doing therapy. This point is particularly important if the individual is calling about couple or family work. Why? Because, as we'll discuss in some detail in later chapters, crucial to any work with couples or families is balance. You don't want to have a long phone session with Carol describing the misdeeds of her husband and expect that Carol won't mention this conversation to her husband before they come in; he'll be starting therapy believing that you have already taken her side.

Finally, if an appointment is set, two questions then arise: Do you send your paperwork ahead of time for clients to fill out? Do you call ahead to remind the client of the time? These are both your call. Some clinicians like to save time by sending out the paperwork; others feel it is an expense that is not recovered if the clients decide not to come. Similarly, some clinicians feel that, like dentists, call-ahead reminders help prevent lost time and money from no-show appointments; others feel that it can be time-consuming and place them in the role of parent. They may compensate by having a clear policy that charges clients for any appointments that are not canceled 24 hours in advance. What is important is that you define your way of working so that clients know what to expect in working with you.

The bottom line, however, on any and all of these various presession contacts is that you present yourself in a professional manner, that you are as responsive and courteous as possible, that you be yourself so potential clients can get a sense of your personality. All this usually gets summed up to what most of us say about first impressions about other professionals in other fields—the doctor, the repairperson: "She sounded nice"; "He sounded fine."

Treatment Maps

A treatment map is the other prep that will help you move smoothly through the first session. This part of your preparation is literally about the first-session state of mind. The idea here is that you mentally have clinical maps at the ready for the treatment of the common problems you are most likely to see: depression, various types of anxiety, common parenting issues, couples and affairs, eating disorders, and so on. With these mental maps onboard you're able to maximize the landscape and impact of the first session. When the client says, at the initial phone contact, that he or she is struggling with obsessive–compulsive disorder (OCD) or binge eating, you already have in mind what you need to do next: what questions to ask in the initial sessions, what to focus on most in sessions, how long treatment may take, whether you need to discuss medication or bringing in family members. Equally important is that by having a treatment map in place, you can clearly lay out for the client in the first session exactly what you plan to do or not do, leaving the client with not only relief but also a clear sense of the next steps.

Be Like a Physician. Think for a moment about your own encounters with your family physician. You wake up one morning with a rash up and down your arm. You look up pictures on WebMD, which only scare you more. You hurry to the doctor. You show her your arm. She looks at it through a magnifying glass. She asks you a series of questions: "When did you first notice this? Does it itch? Were you outside in the last few days? Have you eaten anything unusual? Have you had a fever?"

What the doctor is doing is assessing of course, but also marching through her own mental treatment maps, eliminating or confirming possible diagnoses based on what you say. At the end of the 5 or 10 minutes, she tells you that you have contact dermatitis, probably from being in the woods over the weekend, and here is a prescription for a cream to apply three times a day. If it doesn't start to clear up in 3 days, you need to give her a call.

Do you feel better? Absolutely, because you understand what is wrong and know what you can do to make it better, starting now. And even if the doctor wasn't absolutely sure about the diagnosis, she would have said so—"It could be one of two possible conditions"—and would have still told you what was to happen next—"I'd like you to get a blood test so we can rule out <fill in the blank>. We'll get the blood sample now and have the results by this afternoon and will give you a call." You may be a little more cautious, but you would likely still feel better, knowing that some answer is in the wings.

The point is that you want to be able to do the same as the doctor: Listen to a problem and have a plan to treat it. Will you have to gather more information in the first session to confirm your initial diagnosis, to modify your basic plan? Sure. And like the doctor and the blood work, if you are uncertain or your style is to do an extended assessment process—three sessions of play therapy with a child, for example, before reporting back to the parents—that's generally fine as long as you explain this at the start, whether in the initial phone call or by the close of the first session. Obviously there is not only one way to approach any given psychological problem; what you want to be clear about is *your* way.

Creating Treatment Maps. So how do you go about creating specific treatment maps? Here are some questions to get you started:

- *What is your theory about this problem?* Here you are thinking in terms of your preferred clinical school of thought—psychodynamic, solution-focused, cognitive-behavioral, systems. Each approach conceptualizes problems in specific ways. The psychodynamic approach will examine childhood relationships and coping styles; solution-focused approaches consider what works when things work; cognitive-behavioral, on the connections between thoughts, emotions, and behaviors; systems, on the patterns within relationships. Your approach, with its focus and assumptions, determines all of what comes next.
- *What is the focus of treatment?* This question follows logically from the theory—to develop insight into the past, to

build on strengths, to change thought processes, to track and change behavioral patterns in relationships.

- *What is your focus and how do you explain the process of your sessions?* Obviously, your answer depends upon your preferred clinical approach. For example: "We'll be exploring the past." "I'll be giving you some homework and following up on it." "Our work will be interactive, and I'd like you to come with a clear agenda for the session." "I will primarily listen and make interpretations at critical junctures." "I'll be teaching skills." This information is often what new clients unfamiliar with therapy most want to know about.

- *What do you need to know to complete your assessment?* Before the first session you want to have questions in mind to which you need answers. For example, if you're preparing to work with a family you may want to understand the parents' parenting style, or whether there have been any major changes recently, or the way that arguments in a family unfold. And here you already know that you'll want to see the child alone in a play therapy in the second session.

- *What will be the goals and tasks of the first three sessions?* This is the next-steps question that clients want to know about most, similar to the physician's plan to do the blood work or try the medication for 3 days and then report in. Most clients are used to a process that moves in segments; think about how, after deciding to buy a new car, you scope out cars and get general information before coming back a second time to get details and road test, and maybe coming back a third time to get the okay from your partner and close the deal. In a similar way you want to be able to describe those opening sessions for clients. You know that you'll probably say to the parents that you will see the child for two sessions, then give them feedback about your assessment and propose the next steps; that you'll explain that for the next session you'd like the client's partner to come in as well; that you'll want to spend some time next session exploring family history.

- *When do you need to bring in adjunct services or make changes in format?* What are your criteria for referring a client for a medication evaluation? When in the process might you want to include others—the grandmother, a phone conversation with a teacher, or make a referral for couples therapy? These are the forks in the road, similar to the family physician knowing when to recommend getting a consult with a specialist or going for additional testing. Again, clients like to know these decision points.

- *How long will the treatment last? How do you know when we're done?* Have something in mind so you and the client know what to expect and update as treatment proceeds. For example: "I tend to see clients with this problem for about 10 sessions." "The work is intensive: three times a weeks for 2 to 3 years." "We're done when you can find and hold a job for 6 months . . . when your weight has been stable for a year . . . when the escalating arguments have stopped . . . when you feel better."

Hopefully, these questions give you a better idea of the ground that you ideally want to map out in your mind and what clients are usually thinking as well:

- What is therapy going to be about?
- What is my investment in time and focus?
- What can I expect from you and myself?
- What are the goals and tasks?

To make this process more concrete, let's do a shorthand application of these questions to a clinician's cognitive-behavioral approach to bulimia:

- *What is your theory about this problem?* Bulimia is not about food but about control and managing emotions. Individuals with this problem use food to manage emotions of anger, depression, and anxiety. They often are self-critical, have difficulty being assertive with others; rather than speaking up, they tend to internalize.
- *What is the focus of treatment?* To break the binge-purge cycle around food; to identify triggers and underlying sources of stress; to reduce critical self-talk; to teach assertiveness skills to manage emotions and relationships in healthier ways.
- *What is your focus and how do you explain the process of your sessions?* I'll be giving weekly homework assignments to track specific emotions, to track eating triggers, to teach skills in recognizing specific emotions, to journal about states of mind and critical voices. Sessions will be divided between assessing behavioral changes around food and developing plans to deal with emotional and relationship issues of the week. Clients are expected to come to sessions, to report on homework assignments, and to propose an agenda of issues to discuss. Sessions will be highly interactive with a combination of educational, skill-building, explorative, and supportive components.
- *What do you need to know to complete your assessment?* Explore family history of eating disorders and client's history of past treatment, traumas, use of medication, awareness of triggers. Assess client's willingness to actively carry out homework assignments.

- *What will be the goals and tasks of the first three sessions?* First session: Build rapport, assess history, map out treatment plan. Second session: Provide education on bulimia, teach meditation and emotional tracking techniques, and discuss role of nutritionist. Third session: Bring in significant others (parents, partners) and map out specific ways they can be a source of support in the recovery process.

- *Are there any adjunct services or changes in format expected?* If client does not have a regular physician, ask that she contact one to monitor her medically. Consider possible evaluation for SSRI (selective-serotonin reuptake inhibitor) medication to reduce obsessive thinking and depression. Coordinate with nutritionist and physician. Move toward couple or family sessions, as needed, to resolve relationship issues and practice assertiveness. Consider residential treatment if there is no substantial change in food patterns in 2 months.

- *How long will the treatment last? How do you know when you're done?* Weekly sessions for 3–5 months. If stable, begin to move toward biweekly sessions. If continued stable for additional 3 months, move to monthly sessions for remainder of the year. Treatment can be terminated when client has not engaged in bingeing or purging for 1 year.

Of course, this is therapy, not cut-and-dry computer repair, and so this plan will have to be modified as treatment and events unfold. If the client, for example, breaks up with her boyfriend, she may relapse and need a few months to stabilize and move forward on the plan. If we uncover childhood trauma, such as sexual abuse, 2 months into treatment, or if the medication doesn't seem to be helping, changes in focus and intensity of treatment may need to be modified.

Your next step, if you do not have maps like these in place, is to begin to develop them. You may need to educate yourself, talk with a supervisor, or merely reflect on these questions and see if you can develop a 10-sentence summary of your approach to the common problems you see. With these maps in hand, you are more confident and efficient and better able to present your approach to your clients in that first session.

Skill Set #5: Controlling the Clock

You see this next skill set all the time in sports: Super Bowl games where coaches have players throw passes to save time rather than running the ball; NBA playoffs where players dribble down the court in slow-motion to eat up the clock. The player who controls the clock controls the game. But your family doctor does it too. He knows he has about 15 minutes according to his schedule and insurance reimbursement to get you in and out. On a busy day he's not going to ask how your kids are or whether you too went to that big concert over the weekend. He'll be talking about the problem, his assessment, and his treatment plan—in and out in 15 minutes.

You're less constrained than your doctor, having not 15 but 50 minutes or an hour for your first session. But this doesn't make for a leisurely stroll; you too have a lot to get done. What you don't want to do is let the client talk and talk and shake your head empathically for 45 minutes and use the last 5 to schedule a next appointment. You certainly don't want to spend 20 minutes filling out paperwork and leave clients with a half hour to get their problems on the table. They may do so, but they are going to be resentful. They came with expectations, often similar to the same expectations they have of their doctor who delivers quickly. Sure, therapy may be different, but they better not leave emotionally or mentally empty-handed, and what they do get from this first session better not mimic what they could have gotten at home, online, for free.

Given such circumstances, it's important that you be always aware of the clock and the pacing of the session. Think about the first session divided up into thirds. The first third is about building rapport and having clients tell their stories. You may just let them talk, you may ask probing questions, but your focus here is defining what it is that clients are struggling with and what they expect.

In the middle third, it's about you and what you need to know to make a preliminary assessment. Depending upon your theoretical approach, you may ask about parents, about past medications, about past successes, about past and current relationships. You are gathering information, but you are also tracking the process—being sensitive to any sense of resistance, watching for any transference clues, looking for opportunities to change the emotional climate: "So, can you tell me what you most miss about your mother?"; "You seem distracted right now—what are you feeling?"

The last third is bringing it all home, connecting Parts 1 and 2: the presenting problem with your assessment in order to present your treatment pitch. You need to have enough time for Part 3 so clients do indeed feel that their time was worthwhile, that you are skilled, and that their expectations have at least been partially met. You may not need 15 minutes to do this, but you don't want to leave only 5.

Controlling the clock can seem like a fairly simple and mechanical task of designating a certain amount of time for opening, assessment, and close. But like the other skills sets, what drives this one is leadership, and *active* leadership at that. It's less about the clock and more about your being in charge, shaping the session, moving toward what you consider important to focus upon and discuss while remaining sensitive to clients' needs and expectations.

A tall order. This is what makes the first session difficult, especially if you are relatively new to the field. You can't afford to be passive, to just let unfold whatever unfolds. If you are, what unfolds will be, in clients' eyes, what you have chosen: that it is your style to be passive and reactive. You can't *not* lead; you can only choose to do so deliberately.

So these are the five basic skill sets needed for a successful first session, for what you need to do, independent of your particular theoretical orientation, to ensure that clients leave feeling that this is indeed the Right Product and the Right Person. Obviously, that said, you can carry out all of these skills perfectly and the client decides it's not a good fit after all: He really didn't understand your orientation; something in your appearance reminded her of her father or past boyfriend; you were having a bad day, not feeling well, preoccupied with a personal problem, and missed some of the important cues. You do the best you can do.

To summarize, what *don't* you want to do? You don't want to get too caught up in content and not track the process closely; replicate old wounds and problems by ignoring transference issues; fail to change the emotional climate during the session; not prepare ahead and lose potential clients at the gate or fail to hit the ground running; not watch the clock and fail to cover your goals. Knowing what you don't want to do will lead you to what exactly you *do* want to do. That's what we'll map out in the next chapter: the overall structure of the first session.

CHAPTER 2

Goals for the First Session

IN THIS CHAPTER we are going to consider the structure of the first session, specifically what it is that you need to accomplish by the time the clock runs out. You can think of these as the goals of the session, but also as steps in that we'll discuss them in the order that they unfold within the session process. In the next chapter we'll put this structure in motion and walk through the actual process of the session. Think of this chapter as the playbook; the next, as the game itself.

So, what do you need to do? Here are our seven goals:

1. Create rapport.
2. Identify the client's presenting problem(s) and expectations.
3. Assess and link what you note to the client's presenting problem.
4. Change the emotional climate.
5. Present initial treatment plan.
6. Counter objections.
7. Summarize and explain next steps.

These steps or goals are in a rough logical and clinical order in that you need to do one before moving onto the next. That said, don't think of the first session like an assembly line at an auto factory where parts are added on at each station until the completed car finally rolls off the line. Although some goals have distinct placements, such as presenting the treatment plan, others will run concurrently throughout the session. For example, you'll specifically focus on rapport building at the very beginning of the session, but the rapport building will continue throughout the session by both your deliberate actions and reactions, and by the total impact of the session on the client. Similarly, although you clearly need to set aside a segment of the session to conduct your assessment, confirm your hypothesis, and formulate your treatment plan, you are likely assessing from the time the client sits down or from the time of the initial contact.

So, because you are dealing with people and not machines, the first session is more fluid—a fluidity naturally emerging from the process, which you'll be guiding and tracking throughout the session. It is this tracking that you can always return to when you are making a transition or unsure of where you are going.

The Big Picture

First let's zoom out and look at the larger structure of the first session. As mentioned in the last chapter, it's helpful to think of it in three parts. A quick review:

- **Part 1: Relationship building and identifying problems.** In this first section you lay the foundation by building rapport and identifying the presenting problem and client expectations. You are creating the clinical atmosphere, helping clients feel safe, and gathering or confirming basic information so you can move forward.

- **Part 2: Changing the emotional climate and conducting the assessment.** As mentioned in the last chapter, you want to look for opportunities to change the emotional climate throughout the session, though most often this component occurs in this middle stage. Whereas the first part of the session places the clients on stage, in the assessment it's your turn to step up: Using the client's presenting problems as a starting point, you focus on gathering what it is you particularly need to know to develop or confirm your own hypothesis and the consequent treatment plan.

- **Part 3: Presenting your initial treatment plan, seeking agreement, countering objections, summarizing, and laying out next steps.** This is the point in the session when you need to link the client's primary concerns with your own assessment information to present a preliminary treatment. Once your treatment plan is on the table, you then look for and address any objections that may create resistance and stand in the way of agreement. Once you have the green light, you then summarize and describe what happens next, closing the deal.

Each section has its own focus, and as you move through them sequentially, you make certain that you and the client are in lockstep. You don't move forward until the goals of each section are secure and relatively complete. Again, logically this makes sense—no jumping into assessment until you understand clearly what the presenting problem is—but also emotionally—no diving into assessment or changing the emotional climate if the client feels anxious or seems unclear about your approach. This is where close tracking helps.

If at any point you seem to reach a sticking point—you are doing your assessment, for example, and the client seems disengaged, or you present your treatment plan and the client balks—you need to back up. Likely you have missed something in the previous section; perhaps you failed to build a good-enough rapport . . . or clearly define the presenting problem . . . or gather what you need for the assessment . . . or link the assessment findings to the client's problem.

Let's discuss each of these goals one by one.

Goal #1: Building Rapport

Rapport building is part of Therapy 101: connecting with the new client as the first step in creating the therapeutic relationship. But at some base level rapport is about creating safety and trust . . . about clients feeling comfortable enough with you to relax and let down their defenses, to believe enough in your skill and you as a person to follow you through the session. As mentioned above, you start building rapport from the first contacts— how quickly you respond to their phone call, how you sound on the phone, how well you listen to their initial questions and comments. Like everything else in the first session, you want to be mindful and deliberate, *not* to manipulate for your ends, but to help the understandably anxious person across from you feel at ease. Here are some of the common ways to develop that safety and trust.

Listening

Listening is the most basic skill of all for a therapist. Being quiet, yet alert, allowing the client to get out his story, to say what she needs to say at the beginning of the session without interrupting, is key. Listening, or the lack thereof, is one of the elements that is closely tied to client transferences. Many clients grew up in, or are currently in, relationships in which they were or are ignored, criticized, or dismissed. Discovering in the first moments that you do none of these sets the stage for expecting and creating something different. In the same way, not listening well, even ever so lightly, can trigger old wounds. Triggering such wounds doesn't necessarily mean that clients will bolt—we all have a fairly high tolerance for our childhood emotional wounds—but even with your repairing the relationship, it will take longer to build trust.

Eye Contact

Eye contact is another basic element. We're not talking stare-downs here, just looking at someone square in the eyes. What you want to notice quickly is how much of such eye contact clients can tolerate. Some have virtually no tolerance—they look at their shoes as they talk or make only furtive glances in your direction. Others can tolerate brief instances of contact. You follow their lead: Glance if someone seems shy or submissive, maintain longer eye contact for someone who is less so. You don't want to make the person uncomfortable; on the contrary, you want the person to feel connected.

Along with fostering connection, there is another reason for eye contact, one that you undoubtedly do instinctively: deliberately looking at clients' eyes to assess their emotional state—the eyes as windows of the soul. By watching their eyes, you can read clients' internal emotional climates throughout the session: the client who talks in an animated manner yet has blank or sad-looking eyes; the glances of anger or hurt; the client who seems teary early in the session. You can comment on their eye contact later as a way of consciously changing the emotional climate in the room.

Expertise

Should you ever wind up in an emergency room, you undoubtedly feel more secure knowing that you are talking to the experienced attending physician rather than the intern who looks like your younger brother. The same is true for many clients. By knowing of your reputation through their friends, or having read your profile and credentials and seen your picture online, the stranger-therapist is no longer so strange, your skills no longer so uncertain or mysterious.

But some clients don't use those routes to get to your office. They are referred by their physician, whom they trust, or by an agency, which they don't trust, or they haven't had a phone conversation with you or the time to check you out online. Here is where you presenting yourself and your experience can be helpful. You talk about your years of experience particularly in their areas of concern (e.g., anxiety, couples, PTSD) and you explain your orientation. This is obviously especially important to offset any unsettling first impressions that you know clients may have, such as if you happen to look or be younger than your clients. By countering their assumptions, by letting them know that you have the skill and experience to understand what they are struggling with, you help them begin to relax and open up.

Building Similarities

Good sales people know that customers are apt to like and then buy from those who seem to have something in common with them; similarities build connection. Here are some techniques to consider incorporating into your first session:

Self-Disclosure: Facts about You. Whether and whence to share information about yourself is usually linked to your clinical orientation as well as your own personal style. If you are from a traditional psychoanalytic or psychodynamic school, for example, this is generally a nonissue: Self-disclosure is not part of the therapeutic approach and process. If you come from a different orientation, what you may say about yourself (and when) will depend on your own comfort zone.

Think of self-disclosure as another tool in your clinical toolbox that you deliberately choose to use in the first session as way of building similarity and helping clients relax. Many clients, especially those who have not been in therapy before and have no clear idea about what is to happen, can easily feel "one down"—shy and intimidated by talking to this stranger. By making passing comments about yourself—"When my kids were little," "I used to live there," "I was in the Army myself"—you subtlety help clients see you as a person with experiences similar to their own and underscore your own humanness. Walls are broken down.

Use the Same Sensory Language. The neuro-linguistic programming (NLP) model developed by Bandler and Grinder is now well known, but it was revolutionary when it first came out in the 1970s. Its foundation was the notion that people process experience and information in one of three sensory systems: visual, auditory, or kinesthetic. If you are primarily visual, you think in terms of pictures; if you are more auditory based, sounds of all kinds and spoken words are your focus; if the kinesthetic modality is your comfort zone, then emotions, subjective experience, and literal and figurative touch are your modes of processing. People feel greater rapport when you talk to them in their preferred sensory system. For the visual client who talks in terms of pictures—"What I *see* is . . ."; "What I *visualize* as my goal is . . ."—you use visual images in your session—visual descriptions, diagrams, graphs, and so on. For someone who is auditory—"I *hear* what you're saying"; "The way it *sounds* to me is . . . "—you speak the same language and can rely on lecturettes. For those who are kinesthetic, they will, like the others, speak that language—"I *feel* . . ."; "I can't *grasp* what you're saying"; "I can't *get a handle on* . . ."—so you, too, use kinesthetic sensory language as well as some experiential exercises such as role playing, sculpting, and so on.

There is plenty of information on learning and applying these techniques online to help you refine your awareness and skills. Like other techniques, it is then all about practice—practice that you can do *outside* the office. See if you can decode the sensory system of your brother-in-law, your first-time date, the couple at the next table. When seeing more than one client—a family or couple, for example—try to incorporate all the sensory systems—show diagrams, give lecturettes, do something experiential—in order to build the connection.

Match Body Position, Style of Speaking, and Mood. Body position is also an aspect of NLP. Your client crosses his legs and sits back; you do the same. She crosses her arms and hunches over; so do you. This mirroring of the client is a subtle yet powerful way of building connection. Similarly if you have a client who talks slowly or throws in cuss words, you may want to consider matching his style—talk slowly, throw in a cuss word. This approach also applies to mood—someone who is energetic and talking fast can be matched by your being more energetic and talking more quickly than you normally do.

Dress. In a well-known study, patients were treated by physicians whose verbal feedback was the same, but who differed in their attire. When asked after the appointment how confident the patients were in their doctor, on a scale of 1–10, those doctors who wore a blue lab coat were rated 6.62; those with a white lab coat received a score of 7.25; and those with a white lab coat and a stethoscope around their neck scored 8.82 (Clifford, 2013). Similar studies found similar results (e.g., Rehman, 2005).

Dress is part of first impressions, and again you want to be conscious of your audience here as you are with other aspects of the first session. This doesn't mean that you can't "be yourself" or that you have to show up in construction boots and overalls if your new client is a construction worker. Clients are expecting you to be a professional, so you dress like one. That said, you can tweak your dress for new clients who may be scheduled on a particular day. Dress up and you have more authority. Dress down a bit and you may be less intimidating for certain clients. While the business executive may be more comfortable meeting you in a business suit, the teenager may appreciate a more laid-back appearance. Be sensitive and flexible.

Leadership

This is the final element of rapport building and probably the most important: being in charge of the session. This aspect of rapport building is often a surprise and a challenge for less experienced therapists for two reasons: They associate rapport building with only being a good listener, and because they become flooded with content rather than focusing on process, take a reactive rather than proactive stance.

A lack of leadership—letting clients ramble on, not controlling the clock, not actively changing the emotional climate—not only leaves clients feeling that not much happened and that they didn't get very much for their time and money, but without guidance they also leave feeling unsettled. If you fail to ask the hard questions, for example, clients aren't able to discern the parameters of your style of therapy, what topics are or are not on the table, and whether your personal and professional style can handle deeper issues. If they sense that they have the responsibility of doing the heavy lifting throughout the session, that the pressure is on them, clients stay anxious rather than settling. Your job is to help them step up and set the tone and pace, both verbally—in terms of what topics and issues you do and do not bring up—and nonverbally—what you actively seem to pay attention to and engage in and what you seem to dismiss.

One way of defining your leadership is to liken it to what is described in the parenting literature as the differences among authoritarian, permissive, and authoritative parenting styles. The authoritarian parenting style amounts to control without sensitivity—"Here is what I want you to do—don't ask why—accept it or there will be consequences." Permissive parenting, at the other end of the spectrum, is less controlling, more reactive, and very sensitive and accommodating—"That's fine, Honey"—but fails to provide the clear structure and direction that children need. Authoritative parenting is the solid and the most helpful middle ground—"I know you are upset, but what I would like you to do is . . ."; it is sensitive, proactive, structured (rather than controlling), with continual explanations to the child of what the parent is thinking and why.

You want to take this authoritative middle ground—guiding clients through the session terrain by having the structure of treatment maps at the ready, being sensitive to transference reactions, presenting yourself as confident, proactive, assertive—rather than seeming unsure, reactive, cautious. Clients appreciate, on both emotional and cognitive levels, this type of leadership and the environment it creates. You convey that you know what you're doing while being open and welcoming.

Listening, eye contact, expertise, similarities, leadership—the core elements of rapport building—create the emotional foundation of the session, namely, that of safety. You want to be deliberate, you want to look for signs that the client is settling in, sitting back in the chair, physically relaxing, verbally opening up. You want to apply these techniques throughout the session to maintain connection.

Goal #2: Defining Presenting Problems and Client Expectations

Once they seem settled, it's time to define both the problems that bring clients to your office and their expectations of therapy. Let's take these one at a time.

Presenting Problems

If fostering rapport is the emotional foundation of the first session, clarifying the presenting problems is the cognitive foundation. Presenting problems are the reason clients are sitting in your office; they are your primary focus for everything that comes next. Wherever the session may go over the course of the first-session hour, it needs to return to this point by the end.

Much of this work of defining the clients' problems has likely been started already through your email or phone conversations; clients have talked at varying lengths about their anxiety, eating disorder, or struggle with their spouse. But other clients come in as strangers—those who are referred or simply assigned to you. They come in knowing only your name, and you may know nothing about their presenting problem or, at best, have a one-word label—for example, *depression* or *post-traumatic stress*—jotted down by intake staff.

It's helpful to think of taking the time to determine clients' presenting problems and primary concerns as an extension of the rapport-building process. In her book *Quiet: The Power of Introverts in a World That Can't Stop Talking* (2012), Susan Cain describes Jon Berghoff, now a sales consultant, who started his career in high school selling knives door to door. Even at such as young age, he quickly became a leading seller for the company. Long before he gave his pitch to customers, Berghoff asked numerous questions about their needs and cooking styles. Berghoff is quoted as saying, "I discovered early on that people don't buy from me because they understand what I'm selling; they buy because they feel understood" (p. 238). The same is true for you. By asking the right questions, by drilling down and determining what it is that clients most want or need to change, you not only define your focus, but also help them feel understood and connected.

So it's important that you have a clear understanding of what it is that clients are struggling with most. Often clients will initially present problems in general terms—"I feel anxious around others"; "I get angry at my kids all the time"; "I have a hard time concentrating"—real problems but vague. Your next step is helping them define the problem clearly enough so you know exactly with what you and they are dealing. You might ask:

"Can you give me an example of what you notice when you are anxious around others?"
"When you say that you get angry, what do you actually do?"
"In what type of situations do you have the hardest time concentrating?"

You press for enough information to fully understand what it is that the client most wants to change. This is not about starting your assessment, but about zeroing in on what is most troubling to the person so you can mentally refine your preliminary hypothesis and treatment map.

Of course, there are those clients who come in with not one but several presenting problems: "I feel depressed and have a hard time getting out of bed; I'm also worried that my son is getting in trouble at school, and I'm struggling at work with one of my colleagues." The rule of thumb in these situations, similar to what physicians are trained to do when conducting their initial physical assessment, is to ascertain the client's most pressing concern: "So it sounds like you feel depressed and have a difficult time getting out of bed; you are worried about your son getting in trouble at school; you are having a hard time at work. Of these three problems, what is it that you are most concerned about today?"

This setting of priorities is obviously not to dismiss the other problems but merely to determine where to focus your attention and energy first. Often, of course, problems are psychologically intertwined: The client's depression may be coloring her view of her son or her work colleague or visa versa; her worry about her son and work stress may be creating situational depression. You'll explore these possible permutations further when you move into your assessment.

Again, this section of the session should be relatively short. The goal is to understand what most concerns the client, help the client understand that you understand, and then move forward.

Expectations

Defining clients' expectations involves learning what they envision the process of therapy to be like—long- or short-term treatment, focus on past or present, problem solving, interactive or not, skill training, insight-oriented, behavioral—so that you can clarify your approach and be sure there is a good fit. As with presenting problems, most likely this ground has been covered already—clients have looked at your profile online, have talked to friends who formerly or currently work with you, and you have both talked on the phone or by email—and you've summarized your style and approach, or they have stated what they are seeking as they present their problem: "My wife and I need to learn how to communicate better"; "I have tremendous anxiety before I perform on stage and want to learn ways of calming myself down." Sometimes, however, there was no time during the phone call, or the client was in crisis and was primarily concerned with setting up the appointment. In that case, you'll obviously need to gather this information in the session.

There are a couple of ways of doing this. One is to simply describe your approach at the beginning of the session and look for the nodding of heads or ask if this fits with what the clients had in mind. You can also ask, or clients may volunteer, whether they have been in therapy before and you can ask about their experience and see what they say: "It was good—I had a safe place to talk and she listened"; "It was a waste of time—all I did was talk and he said little"; "He gave me homework that helped me develop the emotional skills I needed." Just as comments about clients' personal relationships tell you about possible transference reactions, comments about past therapists tell you what does and does not work with this particular client, and provide a launching pad for explaining how your approach is similar or different.

You may find that some clients have had no prior experience or even clear knowledge about therapy. They've been referred—by physicians, the courts, social service workers, ministers—sometimes without fully understanding why: "My family doctor gave me your name and said that you could help me with my anxiety"; "I mentioned to my minister how angry I've been getting lately at my teenage son, and he suggested I give you a call."

Your task at this point is to explain both yourself and your services, linking them to the presenting problem:

> "Your doctor has referred other patients to me in the past who have had problems with anxiety. I've helped them learn some skills that they can use to help them calm themselves when they feel anxious. Is this something that you think would be helpful for you too?"

Or:

> "One of the things I specialize in is family therapy. It sounds like you have been having some problems in your relation-

ship with your son. You could both come here together, and I could help you talk about the problems together and see if we could come up with some resolution. How does that sound to you?"

You then look for solid agreement or ask how the client may have been thinking about this appointment differently.

And if you seem to be on different pages—for example, the client's last therapist did body work that the client found especially effective, but you know nothing of this approach—be honest and simply say that you are not trained in body work. Then reiterate briefly how you would approach the client's problem differently, and see if she is willing to give your approach a try, or if not, whether she would want names of other therapists who might provide those services. Even if the client goes elsewhere, she is left with a good impression of your professional integrity.

Goal #3: Assess and Link

Okay, you're up. Whereas the previous goals have focused on the client and laid down the foundation of the therapeutic relationship—rapport building, defining problems and expectations—this goal is all about you. Here is where you do what you need to do to do your job. The client has presented his problem. Now you need to do your assessment, find out what you need to know to construct and present the treatment plan. Obviously what topics you raise, what questions you ask, all depend on your clinical orientation: exploring early childhood, relationships with parents, attachment; tracking cognitions and behaviors; unraveling conversations with family members and sources of emotions; finding what has worked in the past. Again, think about what your physician does after you present your concerns: She begins asking a series of questions—"When did you first notice this? Is the pain constant? Have you eaten anything unusual? Do you feel worse at night?"—to help her link your symptoms to an underlying condition.

What the physician is doing, and you are doing at this point, is not looking for the solution to the presenting problem, but uncovering the problem *under* the problem. You are gathering additional information to help you unlock the possible source of the problem, or to put the problem in a larger context, and thereby fine-tuning the treatment map that you are mentally using as a starting point.

It's helpful, as you conduct this assessment, to keep in mind the client's exact concerns so you can maintain a clear linkage between your assessment questions and the presenting problem. If, for example, George mentions being anxious in large groups, you may want to drill down to the details of those situations: "What do you do to cope? How are groups of strangers different from groups of friends?" This linkage is helpful in two ways: It keeps clients in lockstep with you— they understand where you are going and can relax and join with you in unraveling the problem; and it keeps you from going on autopilot and falling into a generic assessment that doesn't help you fine-tune your treatment map or give you all the information you need, in the allotted time, to present your initial treatment plan.

If, however, your orientation leads you to ask about topics that may seem off the beaten track to the client—details of childhood, for example, or sexuality—be sensitive to the client and make the linkage: "The reason I'm asking you all these questions about _____ is that the way I think <or

what the research shows, or one theory is> about problems such as yours is _____." You're not watering down your assessment for the sake of the client; you are gathering what you need in order to speak the client's language and best address her concerns.

Goal #4: Change the Emotional Climate

Although you're looking for opportunities to change the emotional climate throughout the session, here in this middle section you stay especially alert. The client is more relaxed and your assessment questions—the hard questions, the drilling into details and the past—are more likely to trigger shifts in emotions. Watching the clock, you also still have time to arouse new emotions and settle them before the session is over. So you watch the facial expressions, the eyes, notice the sighs, the sentences that fade off. You gently move in, commenting on what you notice—"You look sad and you didn't finish your sentence: If what?"—and—staying aware of possible transference reactions—you lean forward and talk quietly. How the client reacts to you and adjusts to these shifts in emotion provide further information for your assessment.

Goal #5: Present Initial Treatment Plan

You've gathered the information you needed to confirm your treatment map, and although there is undoubtedly more you would like to know and will discover as treatment moves forward, you have enough for now; you know the direction you both need to go. Here we enter Part 3, the big finish that brings together Part 1—"Here is my presenting problem" from the client and "Here is my approach" from the therapist, and Part 2—"Here is what I understand about your problem"— with now the finale—"Given your problem and my approach, here is what I think we should do next."

Sales people refer to this stage as *closing the deal*. This is where the car salesperson says, for example, "You said you wanted a used car for your daughter, not too many miles on it, safe and under $10,000. I think this car right here is what you are looking for. Only has 40,000 miles on it, has a great safety record, and is only $9,998." This is where your physician says, "You're worried about the rash and you said that it is itchy. Since it's only on that one area of your leg and you said you had gone hiking in the woods 2 days ago, I'm thinking that you picked up a contact dermatitis. I can give you a prescription for a cortisone cream, and that should clear it up in a few days."

You're doing the same. Restating the client's present problem and perhaps his or her expectations and aligning them with your assessment and treatment recommendations:

"So you said you are feeling anxious when you have to make cold calls to customers on your job, and that you are not wanting to take medication, but rather learn some techniques to help you calm yourself. You mentioned struggling with anxiety in high school and college, and could imagine that feeling performance pressure at your job has made this even more difficult. There are several techniques that I can show you next time that you can use in the moment as a first-aid measure, and others, such as meditation, that can help lower your anxiety threshold overall. I'm also thinking that it may be helpful for us to do some role-playing here in the office to help you build up your self-confidence. I'm further wondering if it might be a good idea to ask your supervisor to help you come up with a script that you can follow so that you're not trying to think on your feet each time. How does this all sound to you? Is this what you were looking for? <Or> Does all this make sense?"

And if, after your assessment, you realize that you can't fulfill all the client's expectations, you talk about that as well, explaining your reasoning. This is where the car salesman might say, "While I know you want to keep this under $10,000, given the low mileage that you are looking for, it's going to be difficult to find. This car, for example, is only $8,000 but it has 20,000 more miles on it. This one over here has only 40,000 miles but the Blue Book value is $12,000. This car over here does have the lower mileage and is only $9,000, but it's a subcompact, and I personally don't feel it would be as safe as these others."

The physician's version might go something like this: "I think this is likely to be a contact dermatitis, and the prescription I'll give you should begin to clear this up in a few days. If, however, it doesn't, or if the itching gets worse or you find the rash spreading, I'd like you to come back in and I'll do some blood tests to rule out any possible underlying infection."

Similarly, your response might be something like this:

"I can show you some techniques that you can try. But because this anxiety is affecting your work, if the techniques don't seem to be effective enough after a couple of weeks of practice, I think that you should reconsider talking with your doctor about medication."

Or:

> "While we can certainly talk about some calming tech-
> niques, it sounds from what you've described that some of
> this anxiety is also linked to the fact that you feel intim-
> idated by your supervisor—just bringing it up made you
> feel upset. Confrontation seems to be difficult for you. I
> think it would be valuable to also find ways that you can be
> assertive and let your supervisor better understand what
> you need so this isn't an ongoing source of worry. Does this
> make sense?"

What you are doing throughout this process is again linking
Parts 1 and 2, building on rapport, tying in any changes in
the emotional climate with other assessment information, and
most of all, demonstrating leadership.

Goal #6: Counter Objections and Establish Agreement

If you carefully tracked the process throughout the session,
noticed any verbal or nonverbal objections—the refuting of an
interpretation, an emotional disconnection, a subtle shaking
of the head—and repaired them so that you and the client
stayed in lockstep, your pitch, which is the presentation of
your treatment plan, should go well. Getting yeses all the way
down the line, as we discussed in the past chapter, ensures a
solid closing of the deal. But obviously objections can come
up at this point, in spite of your previous good efforts, simply
because what you offer raises anxiety and questions.

After presenting your plan, you want to wait and see what
the client says next. If he says, "That's sounds good" or "Yeah,

although I'd rather not do medications, I'll think about it and in the meantime we can see how it goes with the techniques" or "You're right about my hesitancy to be assertive with my supervisor, and I agree it's a chronic problem that's just making matters worse and I need to tackle it head on," you move onto the next steps. But you may also hear, "I think learning the techniques is great, but, no, I can't talk to my supervisor about any of this" or "No, no medications, not an option."

Good salespeople know to always anticipate objections. Here are their tips for managing them:

Always Agree and Remain Calm

If you have ever watched a seasoned interviewee—a skilled politician, for example, or frequently interviewed CEO of a company—you'll notice that more often than not their first response to a question, even a difficult one, is positive. They will say something like, "That's a good question" or "I'm glad you asked that" or "You're raising a good point" even if the question implies something negative. When clients raise objections, you want to take the same stance: "I'm glad you mentioned that" or "I can understand your concern," and say it in a calm and gentle voice.

Reduce Anxiety with Consensus

You can counter objections by talking about the experiences of others. This is what the cooking-range salesperson is doing when she says: "I understand that you think you wouldn't use the convection oven and that you don't want to pay the extra cost for it. I've had other customers who thought that they would never use it, but have come back and told me that after they tried it a few times, it really did speed up the cooking time (especially when it's time for that Thanksgiving turkey), browned food evenly, and that they felt the extra cost was well spent."

You're version of this might be to bring similar information:

"While I understand your hesitation about medication, it is something you can try for just a short period of time and see if it makes a difference. If not, you can always stop. I've worked with a number of clients who felt as you do, and most of those who tried the medication felt that even in the short term, it helped break that negative cycle and reduce their anxiety by giving them a greater sense of control."

Or:

"I certainly understand your hesitation about talking to your supervisor, and that's fine with me if you don't want to do that. I've worked with other clients who struggle with confrontation, and though they too were hesitant at first to approach this challenge and learn these skills, they were grateful that they did—they felt it improved their overall self-confidence and ability to manage relationships."

The goal here, obviously, is *not* to manipulate and push clients to do what they absolutely don't want to do; it is about generalizing their concerns and letting them know how others' responses have been different from what they are imagining as a way of reducing their anxiety.

Uncover the Objection under the Objection
What's the problem under the problem? Here you ask: "Just so I can better understand, tell me what concerns you most about medication" or "I was suggesting talking to your super-

visor just so you have more support and clearer guidelines about what you might say to customers. What worries you most about her knowing that you are having a difficult time?"

You can also say what you think the client might be thinking: "Are you afraid that you will become too dependent on the medication?" "Are you worried that talking to your supervisor will make you feel even more vulnerable?" If the client says yes, he is afraid of becoming too dependent on medication, you can educate him on that topic. If he is afraid of getting emotionally overwhelmed when speaking with the supervisor, you can talk about how he can set the pace, role-playing such conversations in the office, and so on, to relieve anxiety.

Make It Easy for the Client to Circle Back
If you encounter solid resistance, stop and make it easy for the client to circle back. "This has been helpful," says George finally. "Let me think about your suggestions, and I'll give you a call." "Fine," you say, "and if you think of any other questions, feel free to call or send me an email." The obvious point here is to avoid having the client feel pressured to do it your way (especially if that is a transference trigger) or feel guilty for saying no. Pressuring only leads to, at best, a short-term passive compliance that eventually collapses, and guilt either does more of the same or makes it difficult for clients to circle back even if they change their minds later.

Goal #7: Summarize and Define Next Steps
Okay, they've agreed wholeheartedly with your plan, or they had questions and objections, but you were able to address their concerns and reduce their anxiety with education, con-

sensus building, and reassurance. It's time to wrap it up. At this point the car salesperson says, "Okay, so you want to go with the $12,000 car with the lower mileage. Let's go inside, talk to the manager, and see if we can do something about lowering that price a bit." The physician says, "I'll have our staff person call in the prescription to the pharmacy within the next hour, and again, if you have questions or if the medication isn't working within a few days, give me a call."

Here you say:

"Okay, let's start with learning techniques, and you can think about the medication and talking with your supervisor. When you come in next week, I'll show you mindfulness, deep breathing techniques, and a brief imagery technique that you can use as first aid when you start to feel anxious. Depending on time, we may be able to do some role-playing here in the office. In the meantime, what I'd like you try to do is notice during the day when. . . . "

There is a value in homework, however brief. It gives clients a sense of fully starting and engaging in treatment, which in itself is therapeutic. It also gives you a way of gauging that engagement. If, for example, you ask the client to just notice what he is thinking about when he starts to feel anxious, and he reports back that he forgot to do it, the forgetting is a bad solution to an underlying problem. You want to wonder if there is a problem in the relationship—he decided that your homework wasn't important enough to do; a problem in the linkage—the client didn't understand the connection between the assignment and his presenting problem; or that your instructions weren't clear or the assignment was emotionally overwhelming. You're not going to necessarily know the answer, but instead ask the questions so you solve the underlying problem.

After the presentation of your initial treatment plan, if you feel that you truly need to do further assessment, say so and map out the short-range course. Here the doctor might say, "I think it is indeed dermatitis, but I'd like to get the lab work before deciding on next steps." Your version is:

> "I think we need to focus on this, but I still have some questions that we unfortunately didn't have a chance to cover. If you don't mind, I'd like to spend next session talking more about _____, and then I can give you better feedback about what our next best steps should be. Is that okay with you?"

Finally, you close the session by mentioning any policy or logistical issues that were not covered in a handout or on your website—for example, parking arrangements, billing, after-hour emergencies, and so on. This shift to "business mode" makes for a good emotional transition—again changing the climate in the room and making it easier for clients to shift back to their everyday lives.

So there you have it: the overall structure of the first session. In the next chapter we will bring this structure to life, drill down into the details, and walk through the actual running of the first session.

CHAPTER 3

Action Steps

The Opening, Middle, and End of the First Session

IN THE LAST CHAPTER we laid out the overall structure and goals of the first session. In this chapter our aim is to bring this structure alive and focus on the choreography of the session. We'll walk through each element of the session.

To do this we are going to track two composite clients in order to show possible variations on the themes. I'll use a cognitive-behavioral framework, fully realizing that you may come from a different orientation. Try not to get caught up in the clinical aspects of these cases, but rather see the clinical material as a medium for describing the first-session *process*. Now let's meet our clients:

- *Emily.* This client leaves a voicemail message saying that she got your name from someone at the student health center at the nearby university. She says that she is a first-year student and is struggling with some "food issues." She is soft-spoken and sounds a bit hesitant. She leaves a phone number, and you phone her when you know you have several minutes to talk, but only get her recording. You hear the same hesitancy in her recorded message that you heard in her call to you. You leave a message encouraging her to look at your website and to call back with any initial questions she may have and her availability for appointments. Finally, after some phone exchanges, you settle on a first-session time.

- *Tom.* This client sends you an email stating that he found you through a therapist resource website, read your profile, and thought this might be a good match. He said he would like to schedule a consultation to discuss ways he could learn to better manage his anger. He signs the email Tom Johnson, yet you notice in his signature line that he is, in fact, Thomas Johnson, PhD, President and CEO, Argon Biologistics, with an address in the city. You call the number on the email and hear his very formal-sounding voicemail message replicating his signature: "This is Thomas Johnson, President and CEO of Argon Biologistics. Please leave a message." As with Emily you encourage him to call or write back with questions, as well as times and days that work with his schedule. You also write the same in an email. He responds by email, and you both settle on an appointment time.

Preparing Ahead

Without reading too much into it, the initial contacts of these two individuals do provide some introduction to who each is: You note Emily's cautious tone, Tom's formal presentation. You're curious how your initial meeting will match these initial impressions. Obviously, each contact with a potential client leaves you with a different impression. There is the older woman who sounds shaken and launches into telling you about the terrible argument she had with her teenage daughter last night and wants an appointment as soon as possible—compared with someone who sounds both polite and matter-of-fact, and who mentions that he got your name from his attorney who suggested he give you a call. And, by the way, he says, there is small time issue and he would really appreciate it if you could schedule something before his court date in 2 days. Each message contains a substantial amount of information.

The shaken mom may cause you to respond quickly and offer support, wonder if she is potentially crisis-driven; the calm and collected gentleman may cause you to hesitate and wonder at his motivation and even potential manipulativeness. You don't need to overanalyze these initial contacts, but simply note them and your reaction. They are part of assessing the client's needs and formulating next steps.

You, unfortunately, didn't have the opportunity to have a phone conversation and gather more information about Emily's or Tom's problems or explain your approach before the session. If you had, you would have been able to find out more about Emily's food issues or clearer details about what Tom may be looking for; but that's fine, you can wait until you meet them. Encouraging them both to look at your website may reduce some of Emily's initial anxiety by seeing that you do, in fact, specialize in eating disorders, and it may provide Tom with more details about your overall approach. By encouraging them to leave questions, you are trying to eliminate any of those preliminary make-or-break issues that clients sometimes have. For example:

"Do you take my insurance?"
"Do you have a sliding fee scale?"
"Can I have the same day and time each week?"
"If I can't find a babysitter, can I bring my baby?"
"I may at some point want to bring my partner in, is that okay?"
"Do you do psychological testing?"

The answer to many of these types of questions are cut and dried: You do take their insurance or you don't have a sliding fee scale; you generally can set aside the same day and time but probably not for a couple of weeks; babies—no, or we can try and see; you can do a clinical assessment, but if they are looking for a formal paper-and-pencil psychological testing, you can refer them to someone who does.

Others require some explanation: Yes, you are comfortable having partners come into a session, but there is that question of providing balance and being clear what the goal of doing so is—to provide a forum for a one-session discussion on a particular topic or to shift to couple therapy? You want to answer briefly on the phone or in an email and see if that settles the client's anxiety. You can save further discussion for the first session.

Now is the time to begin to speculate about your new clients and mentally map out your initial treatment plan. Let's take them one at a time.

Mental Map of Emily

This client is a freshman in college, 18 or 19 years old, in a time of major transition and stress for many this age. Not only do these new college students need to learn how to manage the difference between college workloads and those of high school (irregular day schedules, no daily assignments, classes a couple of times a week instead of daily, big important papers and finals), there is also the moving away from home, getting oriented to dorm life, dealing with sorority/fraternity rush, making new friends, and for most probably finding plenty of opportunities for drinking, partying, possibly drugs.

Food Issues. Anorexia, binge eating, bingeing and purg-ing? At this point you don't know, but you're already pulling together a general treatment plan: Emily is motivated to both go to student health and to call you—good. Is this a new prob-lem or an old one that has been ongoing or in remission but triggered by stressful changes? You need to explore history—about eating and stress patterns, whether she has been in treat-ment in the past, what has worked or not worked, whether she is on, or has taken, any medications.

She sounds hesitant on the phone. You know that those who struggle with eating disorders often have an accommoda-tive, internalizing, sometime perfectionistic personality. She is also calling a stranger whom she knows is older than she—possible considerations for transference issues.

And then there is your own treatment map for eating dis-orders. In addition to the history and nature of the problem, you need to look at specific triggers, how ingrained the food patterns are, any underlying trauma, questions of medical sta-bility, and need for a nutritionist to help develop a meal plan. And then there are the possible personality dynamics: Does she, in fact, internalize emotions? Is she self-critical and per-fectionistic? Does she have difficulty with confrontation? Is she aware of her eating disorder voice? Can she tell when she is feeling vulnerable and needs to be careful with food? Does she acknowledge that she has an all-or-nothing mindset?

What do you need to know most by the end of this first

session? Obviously what type of eating disorder she has and how severe it seems to be, whether it can be handled successfully on an outpatient basis, whether you need to recommend a nutritionist and medication consult. What was her past treatment, if any, and what helped and didn't? Does she have some understanding and insight into her problem or is she starting from ground zero? Why is this issue all coming together now? That's enough to get you started.

Mental Map of Tom

Just as you have a preliminary map for treating eating disorders, you have one for anger management. It's about clients learning to identify triggers, be aware of their changing emotional states, acquire concrete ways of self-regulating when irritation and anger begin to climb, and deal effectively with stress. It's also about personality. Anger is often about control and underlying anxiety, a learned hypervigilance, a self-critical mindset. Treatment focuses both on the self-regulation and the underlying emotions and issues. Start with self-regulation and move toward the others.

Unlike Emily, who is more likely to blame herself, you know it's common for those who struggle with anger to blame others for creating their anger, which makes it difficult for them to realize and take responsibility for the problem. Is Tom coming because he is, in fact, concerned about his behavior, you wonder, or has someone, such as his partner, pushed him into it and he is merely accommodating her either to relieve the tension or to get her off his back? Has he been in therapy before, and if so, did he find it helpful?

As with Emily, are there certain triggers for Tom's anger? When he gets angry, how bad does it get—does he get physical or solely verbally enraged? Can he catch himself and calm himself down, or does he go from 0 to 60 in nanoseconds without any awareness? Can he cope at work, but blow up at home? Is Tom the type of person who internalizes and accommodates and finally blows up, or is he constantly irritable with things worsening lately? Is he aware of other emotions—does he have an emotional range (sadness, worry, frustration, fatigue)—or, like many with anger issues, is anger the only primary emotion that he is able to express? Does he come from a chaotic or abused childhood, and as a result is he wired to always be on edge, anxious and hypervigilant? Does he have ways of reducing stress? Have there been any unresolved losses that have possibly fueled his anger recently?

And just as Emily may have her own issues with authority, so may Tom. He is a CEO of a company, obviously a motivated individual, and you can imagine him being someone who is comfortable being in charge and used to having others respond quickly to his concerns and directives. If he has not been in therapy before, you wonder how will he deal with not being in charge and having less power and control? Does he expect that process to be similar to work and see you as an employee, or can he take a more rounded perspective?

What do you need to know by the end of the first session? Tom mentioned that he is setting up a consultation. Does that mean that he is shopping around, using this as a meet-and-greet screening session, seeking a one-shot clinical assessment? What are his goals for the session and for therapy? What is the nature of his anger—how volatile is he, how often, and in response to what triggers?

There are obviously other questions and other ways to frame your thinking, depending on your clinical model. The point here is that you are already working, already anticipating what it is you need to cover in the session in order to confirm or disconfirm your speculations, structure your assessment, and help you map the treatment plan that you will present.

Okay, you're ready. Time to walk through your first sessions with these clients.

Part 1a: Opening (5–10 Minutes)

Upon her arrival in your office, Emily begins by apologizing for being late. She had to catch the bus from campus and didn't realize how long the walk would be from the bus stop. She's really, really sorry.

"That's okay," you say.

She sits back. "I really like your office." Her voice sounds similar to that voice message, a little bit on edge. You copy her body position and ask if she had a chance to look at your website. "Only briefly," she says, "crazy week."

"That's fine. Let me just take a minute to introduce myself." And you do—telling her how long you have been in practice, where you worked before, and deliberately mentioning your experience treating eating disorders. Your goal at this point is to give her time to settle, to get used to your voice, to reduce her anxiety about you and the process.

For Tom the opening process would be much the same—looking for the contrast between your initial impressions and his presentation in the session—the all-business CEO, authoritative, perhaps a bit stiff, or something more casual. You might ask about the nature of his company, you might dress up more for Tom, doing the suit to be able to match his possible expectations or his attire. And just as you mention your background with eating disorders to Emily, you would do the same with Tom—talking about your experience with anger management. Keeping in mind his PhD, you might consider underscoring your clinical and academic experience in your introduction—papers, presentations, research—especially if you are younger than he, knowing that whatever impressions you don't try to create, he will fill in with his own.

"Have you been in therapy before?" you ask Emily. By the question you can find out about her therapy experience, her impressions of it, gain some perspective of her psychological history, and have a platform for further defining your own approach.

"Yes," she says, "a few years ago. I had a breakup in high school and coped, I suppose, through restricting. I was losing weight. My mom got concerned and took me to a woman therapist."

"How was that experience?" you ask.

"I guess okay. She really didn't say much. I talked about my boyfriend. Went for a couple of months. I guess I felt better just because I got over him, stopped restricting, then I stopped going."

She is sounding more relaxed. Obviously, you're listening to both what she is saying and more importantly, for what she is *not* saying. What you heard is that she has, in fact, used restriction as a way of coping with an emotional crisis and that she doesn't have a long history of anorexia or of treatment. What she is not saying is anything noteworthy about her past therapist (she didn't even mention her name), or any particular focus on the eating disorder itself—no mention of learning about triggers, working on meal plans, or identifying her eating disorder voice. Her takeaway seems to be that she largely improved because she recovered from the loss, albeit by talking about it with the therapist, and with this change the eating disorder fell away.

Here is your opportunity to compare and contrast your

own approach: "Did you feel what your therapist did was helpful?" you ask.

"Well, like I said, she didn't say much. It did give me a safe place to talk about how I was feeling."

"There are many different therapy approaches, and it sounds like your previous therapist used a nondirective approach where she let you set the pace and topic. My style is a bit different. Although I think it is important for you to have a safe place to talk about what's on your mind, I also think of us as a team working together to solve your problem. I tend to be behavioral, focusing on things you can do between sessions to better understand your thinking and behaviors, and to experiment with changing them. How does this sound to you?"

"Actually, that's great. I like the idea of knowing what I can do differently. I don't want to just talk about stuff."

You are tracking. Did her "that's great" seem emotionally sincere, or did it sound less solid, perhaps because Emily's transference issues are being triggered and she is accommodating? If solid, you move on. If her "that's great" sounds shaky, you may want to clarify: "You say that this is a good idea, but you sound a bit tentative to me. Is there anything about my approach that concerns you?" You speak in a gentle and calm tone.

If she says no, this seems like a good approach, you march ahead. If it is a yes, but with still some edge of caution in her voice, you decide to move on for now, so that you both don't get bogged down and so you don't ramp up her anxiety by focusing on a small issue so early in the session. You'll be tracking throughout the session, and she'll have a clearer picture of your style when you present your treatment plan. If she says "Yes, I guess I wondering what types of things I would need to do between sessions," you have a wonderful opportunity to clarify your style, answer her concerns, and find that she is more assertive than you may have originally thought.

Like a skilled poker player who spends the first few hands uncovering the other players' "tells," at this point in the game you too are trying to read Emily's emotional patterns—how open or closed she is, how she both displays and manages her anxiety in the room, the language she uses—all are part of understanding the personality and learning style of your client. By noting and asking about her reactions to your comments, you are also teaching her about your approach: that it is interactional, that how she feels in the room and with you is important, that you are sensitive to her reactions. And even if this is difficult for her to manage in these opening minutes, she is also experiencing the way your form of therapy is different from her past experience.

When you ask Tom about his past therapy experience, let's suppose that he says that he has never been in therapy before. "I remember you saying that you found me online and thought that this might be a good fit. I'm just curious about why you thought that?"

"Well," he says, "you mentioned that you do CBT. I don't know a lot about it, but actually my wife saw someone a few years ago who used that approach and she found it helpful. And you said that you tended to focus on the here and now and taught techniques. I'm a getting-it-done kind of guy and that's what made me think that this might be a good fit. I'm looking for things I can do when I start to get upset."

Tom just did a good job of laying out his expectations for therapy. You are both on the same page and good to go. If Tom were less clear—say, a friend of his had given him your name, but he had no idea how this worked—you would be taking time to explain your approach and would be asking if this is what he had in mind. Again you would be tracking process—a weak "That sounds fine" needs to be clarified and challenged, whereas the sturdy "That's what I had a mind" gives you both the green light.

And what if it turns out that the client's expectations don't match your style? Emily says that she actually found her first therapist's approach extremely helpful; Tom thought his wife's CBT experience was a lot of superficial mumbo jumbo and he is actually looking for someone trained in Jungian analysis. You define but do not defend your approach; you describe the way you think about presenting problems differently; you explain what the focus would be and what sessions would look like. As any good salesperson would do, you compare and contrast your product against others, pointing out the merits of yours . . . and then leave it to them. Although such surprise mismatches can occasionally arise with a referred client who comes only knowing your name, or a mandated client who is coming under duress and often doesn't care whom he sees because he really doesn't want to see anyone, such surprises are likely to be rare, given the Internet and your own preparation and outreach.

These opening moves are about rapport, about creating that platform of safety. Sensing that Emily is possibly self-critical and self-conscious, you intentionally reassure her that it is okay she is a bit late, you match her emotional range, you monitor her anxiety, and you deliberately set out, by your questions and tone, to show her how you do therapy and how it is different from her past experience. And although Tom has a different presentation that you'll need to mirror, the message and tracking are the same. You're clarifying expectations, removing any large obstacles—ensuring that you have your first yes, that the client is comfortable with you and your approach—before moving forward.

Part 1b: Client Story (10 minutes)

"Tell me, how can I help you?"

Some clinicians have clients fill out a checklist or questionnaire before the session, which they may look over at this point and ask questions. Others may ask some preliminary background questions—married, how long, kids, ages, ever taken psychotropic medications?

But at some point you need to turn the corner and ask about why they are there. Often clients will say that they don't know where to start; spouses/partners or family members will look at each other: "You start," "No, you start." You just wait, remaining relaxed. If the client really seems to be struggling, you can say, "Start anywhere," or "You mentioned that you were having a problem with _____."

Emily, however, jumps right in. "As I mentioned before, I was anorexic, I guess, for a few months in high school. *(Did her previous therapist not define and clearly talk about anorexia?)* I was a bit worried before I started this year with the stress of college and all, but I've been doing okay. But then my mother got sick. *(Pause; you notice that her eyes are getting red, her voice a bit quieter.)*

"I'm sorry. What's wrong with your mother?" *(Asking details to tap into emotions).*

"She has a breast tumor that looks to be cancerous. The doctors want to remove it, but aren't sure what they want to recommend next: lumpectomy, mastectomy? They need to do more tests." *(Again a pause.)*

"Oh, I'm so sorry to hear that. How are you doing with this?"

"It's been hard. My mom and I are close and I'm an only child" *(eyes getting red again)*. "Anyhow, I noticed that I'm falling back into my anorexic ways, like high school—worrying about what I'm eating, restricting, counting calories, feeling fat. . . . "

"Have you lost weight?"

"A few pounds."

She's defining the problem—anorexic behaviors triggered by her mother's possible cancer, similar to what happened with the breakup from her boyfriend. You obviously want to toggle back and forth, finding out more about her coping with her mother's condition and her anorexic behaviors. For now you decide to ask questions about the anorexia—triggers, good days, bad days, whether she can override her behaviors with self-talk, is she aware of when she is being self-critical, how does she do eating around others, does she ever binge?— just so you can get a clearer picture of this aspect of the presenting problem.

That's the content. How's the process? So far, you are in lockstep. She's thought through what she wants to say and is not getting derailed or more anxious as you ask your questions. There is the reddening of her eyes, indicating understandably strong emotions about her mom. You could pick up on it now—say you notice that she seems to be feeling a bit upset right now—but you wait so she can get her story out and not get overwhelmed. You can circle back to this during your assessment.

Tom too speaks right up. He actually sits right up as well, you notice, as though ready to give a speech, and he does:

"So this situation came up last week at work that concerned me, which is what prompted me to write to you. While I admit I run a fairly tight ship at work, I believe I'm always professional around my employees. Well, an incident came up last week with one of my project managers—details aren't important—but I just blew up. Was screaming at the guy! He was stunned, and I guess I was too. After chewing him out, I stomped away. I was able to get back to my office and eventually calm myself down. Of course, I then went and apologized to the guy.

"When I told this to my wife that night, she was supportive, but she also said that she noticed that I had seemed more irritable of late. That surprised me, but after she said it, I realized she was right. But I don't understand why I flew off as I did with my employee, and I can't have that happening again. You can't afford to act like a jerk when you're in charge of the business." He stopped, speech over.

"It sounds like this was understandably very upsetting for you. I'm wondering, when you look back on the incident at work, or even about your wife's comment, how do you make sense of it?"

"Well, I have been working hard to make the deadline for a grant proposal and we're having some cash flow problems lately."

"Cash flow problems?" (*making language clearer*)

"Yeah, that's part of every business. But to answer your question, yes, I guess I've been stressed. Not sleeping all that well. My mind's always busy with something."

He's not opening up about business, you notice. Because you are a stranger, and not yet trustworthy? Because it's a replication of the problem—internalizing his emotions—and what he does most of the time? He did open up to his wife, but whether this is standard fare or not is too early to tell. "Have these blowups happened before?"

"I guess. About 6 months ago I snapped at an employee—nothing like last week—but clearly unprofessional. I thought I was probably tired and, of course, I apologized and cleared things up."

Your mind is working. In terms of treatment plans, Emily, in your mind, is fairly clear—she is defining a specific problem—her anorexic behavior—and a specific stressor—her mother's health. You need to focus on both, and since she hasn't had any previous experience with a focused treatment of anorexia, this is a path you both need to take. Tom is less specific—he has periodic anger outbursts, is under stress, is displaying the same "professional" behavior with you that he keeps talking about on the job—not openly anxious, but stiff, less open, possibly less insightful. Although you feel that there are no major obstacles to overcome at this point with either client, you realize that there is a challenge with Tom, finding a way for him to relax more and change the emotional climate.

Part 2: Assessment (15–20 minutes)

So Emily is emotionally struggling with her mother's cancer and her anorexic behaviors, Tom with his angry outbursts. The problems are clear in your mind; there is no vague talk of "food issues" or "getting upset." If you were unsure, you'd ask for more description so you'd know exactly what it is the client is most concerned about and wants help with.

It's time for you to gather the additional information you need to verify your clinical hypothesis and solidify your treatment plan. Here you draw on your own clinical theories—

CBT, psychodynamic, object relationships, narrative—that guide your questions and focus, keeping in mind that you need to link your information to the client's primary concern. You are also looking for further cues about transference issues, opportunities to change the emotional climate, and, as always, watching the clock.

So what more do you need to know from Emily? You have an initial map of her eating patterns, as well as her awareness (or lack of awareness) about the connection between food and emotions. You track this further: Can she tell first thing in the morning when she is vulnerable to restricting? When she is particularly worried about her mother or has a conversation with her, does it seem to immediately affect her eating? Is what she is doing now different from what she did when she struggled with the boyfriend breakup?

And as you considered in your preparation, you also ask about the broader aspects of her personality and coping style: Does she have ways of managing stress? Is she perfectionistic, self-critical? What does she do when she gets angry? Does she have friends at school? You are also wondering about outside sources of support and what's not being said. She didn't mention her father, so you ask about him.

"I'm wondering about supports for you. You haven't mentioned your father. Where's your dad? Do you see him? Are you close to him too?"

"No, not really. Though my parents aren't legally divorced, they've been separated for about 5 years. They have almost no contact with each other. My father moved to Florida, where he is originally from, after they separated. We don't get along that well. He was always pretty critical of me. I felt like I could never please him. We talk on the phone occasionally— he asks about school. It's all fairly stiff and polite."

You note her mention of his criticism, undoubtedly her sensitivity to it, and her coping by keeping away. You need to be careful that you don't inadvertently trigger her feelings of criticism in her relationship with you. You also note that she was a young teen when her parents separated, and you wonder if being an only child may have caused her to step up and be a support and confidante for her mom.

Throughout this assessment process Emily has seemed open and has stayed relaxed. It's time to circle back to the mother and her cancer. "And does your mom live close by?"

"She's about 3 hours away."

"And do you get to see her?"

"I've been going home the last few weekends, and we talk every day on the phone."

"I bet your worry about your mom's cancer can feel overwhelming for you at times."

"It sure is. I think about it all the time."

"What is it you're most afraid of?" You know that the answer is obvious, but your intention is to now tap into those deeper emotions.

"I'm so afraid that she might die." Again, you note the reddening of the eyes; she looks down.

"You're looking really sad right now."

"I guess I am." And the tears start. Not heavy sobs but the quiet crying. You pass her the tissues and you sit and wait.

Although the overall picture of Tom is less clear than that of Emily, your goal is the same: to gather whatever information you need, based on your clinical model, to connect the psychological dots and construct or confirm your treatment plan. Because anger is partly about self-regulation and also a bad solution to something else, you begin your exploration on both fronts. You ask Tom how he handles stress—he plays golf when he can; whether he has taken meds—he did a long time ago, back in college, when he was having a hard time with stress, but gave it up after about a month because he didn't like the side effects, which made him feel not himself, and no, he doesn't remember the name of the medication. You ask if he uses alcohol. He says, "One, maybe two drinks tops, at night"—helps him relax. Children? Two kids, one in college, one a senior in high school. Actually used to help out with coaching soccer, but that was before he started his company. Wife—great—good relationship. All with the same authoritative clip in his voice.

You ask about his childhood and he starts to answer at the same pace and tone. Both parents were alcoholics; he is the oldest of 3 kids. He had to step in a lot; often wound up making dinner because parents couldn't; helped younger sibs with homework. Parents argue? Usually not, but there was tension and a few times they really did have big blowups.

"How'd you cope?" you ask.

"Stayed alert, did what I needed to do, tried to stay under the radar. My younger brother never could do that." *(He shakes his head, looks down.)*

"I notice you're shaking your head. What are you thinking?"

And now his voice shifts. "When he became a teenager, my brother started taking my dad on, picking fights. They had some big ones. Sometimes I'd try and jump in, but that only made matters worse—my father would get even angrier."

"How's your brother doing now?"

"He eventually wound up in prison. For stupid shit."

He shakes his head again; the tone in the room has changed, softened, quieted. "Is he still there?"

"No, he got out. But he's an alcoholic like the old man was. I don't like going down that road."

And you don't—that may come later. What's important is that the emotional climate has changed; Tom has lowered his defenses, showed some vulnerability. He also told you about his overresponsibility, coping by being good; like kids in a lot of alcoholic families, he's probably wired to be hypervigilant, always anxious, always on edge, countering it with control of himself and everything around him.

"Just wondering, how do you do with transitions? What I mean is, are you a kind of guy who tends to plan things out—what you're going to do during the workday or weekend, for example—and can get rattled if things don't go as planned?"

"I guess you could say that. I know my wife would say I do. If she tells me at the last minute that she invited her mother over for dinner on Sunday, I get irritable, not because I don't like my mother-in-law and don't want her to come over, and not because I think my wife should ask for my permission or anything like that, but because I had something else in my mind that I was planning to do, so I get a bit upset."

"And I'm guessing that you hadn't mentioned to your wife ahead of time what you were planning."

"Yep, you're right."

Part 3a: Presenting the Treatment Plan (5–10 minutes)

The clock is ticking. Do you have what you need to move forward? If not, too bad. Time to move forward.

But you're actually in good shape. You've gathered what you need to know about Emily's anorexia, her personality, and her worry about her mother. And ditto for Tom—compared to where you started the session, you can connect the dots in terms of his internalization, hypervigilance, and control issues. Basically what undergirds his anger, you believe, is stress and lots of anxiety.

Most importantly, perhaps, the climate has changed. Emily was willing and able to share some of her sadness about her mother—an indication not only of her level of emotion but also a sense of safety with you. And Tom, although not so dramatic a shift, was able to lower his guard, which is significant for someone who has not been in therapy before and is used to being in charge.

It's time to present your treatment plan.

Emily's Treatment Plan

"I appreciate your coming in and being open with me about all that you've been struggling with. Let me tell you what I'm thinking, and you see how it sounds to you.

"Understandably, your mom's illness and the uncertainty about it have been overwhelming for you. As you said, you both are close, and I could imagine that being an only child, and with your parents' separation, it's easy for you to feel a special connection to your mom and even a sense of responsibility for her. I'm worried about the anorexia, as are you. It can be a difficult illness to manage. Although your mind focuses on food, what you are actually doing is trying to manage your emotions. If you have difficulty expressing your emotions—and you did say that you have a hard time with confrontation and disappointing people—if you feel like you walk on eggshells a lot or put pressure on yourself to always do well, that's a lot to handle under the best of circumstances. Now with your mom's illness, with your having no control over it, with your being worried and maybe feeling a sense of responsibility for her, it's easy for the eating disorder to kick in—you control food when it's hard to control anything else. Is this making sense?"

"It sure is." She nods her head. It's a clear, solid *yes*.

You then go on to explain that you want to support her as she copes with her mom's illness, but you also want her to get focused on treating her anorexia. You tell her that you'd like her to hook up with a doctor at student health who can check her medically. You'd also like her to talk to the doctor about medication—an SSRI—to help her not only with her worry about her mother, but to also help her with her obsessing about food. This addition will help her break her automatic patterns. You'd also like her to consult with a nutritionist to help her come up with a meal plan—both to help her get the nutrition she needs and to increase her weight, but also to give structure to her meal planning and reduce her anxiety about it; she can just follow the plan, rather than getting tangled up trying to make decisions. If there is not a nutritionist on staff at student health, tell her you can give her names of professionals in the community.

Again, you ask, "Does this make sense? How does this sound to you?"

And she nods her head. Throughout your speech you watch to see if she is staying engaged, not getting overloaded with too much information. It seemed like she was attentive. Here you are making sure that she has not fallen into accommodation and made pleasing you her priority.

"Do you have any questions about anything I've suggested?"

"Actually, no, I feel a lot better. Having a plan, knowing what to do really helps, and it all makes sense." You feel confident that she is, in fact, onboard.

Now let's turn to Tom:

"Before we run out of time, I'll like to tell you what I'm thinking."

"Sure," says Tom, "that's what I want to know."

"You're worried about your angry outburst, and it seemed like it surprised you. Some people are angry or irritable a lot of the time, whereas others tend to be unaware of it, and then every once in a while it all comes out and they go from 0 to 60 in nanoseconds. It sounds like you might be more that type."

"I'd say so."

"It actually makes sense to me. You mentioned that both your parents were alcoholics. That's a difficult environment for children to live in because they never quite know what's going to happen next. It's common for them to feel like they are walking on eggshells. They're always watching how much Dad or Mom drink, what kind of mood they're in. They become hypervigilant, where they're always on guard, always looking to see what come next."

"That makes sense."

Tom's with you. "You also have to learn to cope with the tension and stress. You don't have many options as a kid. You can also get angry, like your brother did, or withdraw and hide out in your room all the time . . . "

"That was my sister. That's what she did."

"Or, especially if you're the oldest, like you, you can get *good*—you step up, take responsibility, and, as you said, stay under the radar. When you do that, you learn a couple of things. You learn to depend on yourself, rather than others; to be good and responsible all the time; and to internalize your emotions, to hold them in, because it's not safe to let them out. And if your dad had a temper and blew up a lot, it makes sense that you instinctively figured out what you would need to do to *not* be like him—and to not be like him meant being responsible and not getting angry. Does this make sense?"

"Yep, I'm with ya."

"You also mentioned that you have a hard time with transitions, getting rattled if plans change, as when your mother-in-law came for dinner when you weren't expecting her. That too makes sense. The folks who often go from 0 to 60 are not just holding in emotions like anger, but underneath they are often anxious most of time. They manage their anxiety through their efforts to control themselves and others, but it's the anxiety that comes to the surface when things don't go as planned. To those around them, it often comes across as irritability. Again, does this make sense?"

"So you're saying that my outbursts are because I'm stressed and hold emotions in, and that my anger is actually anxiety?"

"Yeah, that's basically what I'm saying. Usually what worked for you as a child doesn't work as well in the bigger adult world. You have more people to worry about besides your parents and teachers, and the anxiety and hypervigilance that drive you to push yourself and accommodate many others causes a lot of stress. It's easy for you to start to feel like the martyr and to have growing resentment because you're doing so much and not being appreciated for it; then suddenly, little things trigger the explosion."

"Wow. That's makes a lot of sense. I never thought of my anger, or my control, for that matter, as tied to anxiety, but I can see that now. That's why my head is probably always running a hundred miles an hour."

Tom's onboard. You've connected the dots for him by linking his presenting concern with what you learned about his childhood and presenting a concise explanation for his behavior. You now move ahead to talk about your treatment plan. You explain that you want to focus on two areas: (1) self regulation—helping him to better recognize and monitor how he feels, so things don't build up inside him, and to learn ways to calm himself when they do (these are the techniques that he asked for); and (2) emotional wounds—helping him upgrade that childhood software (the computer analogy resonates with his professional tasks and language) by considering ways to be more open with others and use them for support, to counter the drill sergeant in his head, experiment with being less driven, and push back against the control that his anxiety stirs.

Part 3b: Countering Objections (5–10 minutes)

Although Tom is onboard with your plan, you add another possibility at the end: "And I'm wondering if you might want to consider trying some medication."

Tom stiffens. "What for?"

"Well, if we're agreeing that some of this is underlying anxiety and because you said that you are going through a particularly stressful time now with the grant proposals, medication can help reduce your feeling of anxiety and worry."

"But I tried it before and I didn't like it."

"I understand. But that was a long time ago, and there are many more and different medications out there."

"I don't like drugs."

"That's fine. I'm only suggesting this because many people have found that it helps break their behavioral and emotional cycle; they are less apt to fall into autopilot and better able to put into place what we've talked about doing. If you are worried about becoming dependent on medication, and have to take them for forever, you don't need to worry. You can try them and when you don't need them anymore or because you don't like the side effects, you can stop whenever you want; you only need to check with your doctor so she can let you know how to go off them medically. But usually you need to give them more than a couple of weeks to get over the initial side effects."

"Okay, that makes sense. I'll think about it."

"Great. I'll show you the self-regulation techniques first next time, and that may be all you need. I'm just mentioning it as something to consider."

"Fair enough. Thanks."

What happened here? Well, you were countering objections, and it happens to be the same objection you encountered in the last chapter with George. And as with him, you remained calm. You didn't argue. You explained your thinking and you brought in consensus wording—"many people have found." And you're not surprised by his reaction. He mentioned that when he tried meds in college, he didn't feel like himself. It makes sense that this was rattling for him— he probably worried that the medication would affect his sense of control. That's why you mentioned what he might have been thinking—namely, that he would get hooked. You tried to reassure him that he did, in fact, have control.

Unlike Tom, Emily didn't have objections, though you were again alert to the possibility of her easy accommodation. You'll have to see how things evolve over the next weeks with her. Is she able to follow the week's plan that you both map out, or does she struggle? And if she does struggle, is it because the steps you are asking her to take at this point are too large, or because she was only accommodating you and not fully onboard. You'll find out.

Part 3c: Summary and Next Steps (5 minutes)

You're on the home stretch with only a few minutes left. You know that the clients are onboard, both in terms of the relationship and the treatment plan you've proposed. You've been specific about what you will focus on in sessions, and over the course of this first session they have learned about and become more comfortable with your clinical style. Time to wrap it up.

Wrapping Up with Emily

"It was really good meeting you today. How was this for you?" You ask the question as a way of stepping back and having you both reflect on the larger process of the session.

"This was really helpful. Though I don't know what's going to happen with my mom, I feel hopeful. I feel I can get through this." Again, she seems sincere.

"Great. I appreciate your openness. So, let's talk about next steps."

And here you reiterate her going to student health, getting an appointment with a doctor, and seeing if they have a nutritionist on staff. If not, she is to give you a call and you'll give her some referrals. You also give her some assignments to track her emotions and eating patterns for the next week. You schedule the next appointment and hope she gets some more information about next steps with her mom. She thanks you. You consciously do not say anything more about her mom. You don't want to stir up her sad emotions about her mom again as she leaves.

Wrapping Up with Tom

"I want to thank you again for coming in. So you initially thought this might be a good fit—do you think it is?"

This is that same step-back question you asked Emily, but in Tom's language.

"Yeah, I really think so. Again, I haven't done this before, but what you've said has made sense." You notice that he is adopting your language—"makes sense"—a good sign.

"I'm glad. Okay, so here's some homework for you to do. . . ."

And you give him some assignments to track his emotional state every hour and to ask himself if he is notices when he starts to get worried or irritated and what might be going on. He doesn't have to do anything at this point, just notice. He can think about the medication, and if he wants, go online and read information about medication and anxiety. You also mention that if, at any time, he would like to bring his wife in, that is fine with you. You schedule another appointment and shake hands.

You obviously see how Emily and Tom are similar in many ways—that only child–oldest sibling personality, the internalization, the anxiety, the use of control. But they are also different: Emily is in a situational crisis and more accommodative; Tom is struggling with longer-standing coping styles.

What you have tried to do with both is accomplish the goals of the first session: Build rapport and help them feel safe; define their presenting problems and expectations; do your own clinical assessment and link it to their presenting problems; propose an initial treatment plan; counter any objections; and summarize and define next steps. You've moved through the three parts of the first session—the opening with rapport and problem defining—the middle with assessment—the closing with the treatment plan and summary. And you've accomplished it all within the session hour.

Again, your own content with these clients may be vastly different: different questions, perhaps more focus on childhoods, different ways of mapping the treatment plan and next steps. What is important is the *process*: being able to monitor what happens in the room closely, changing the emotional climate—with Emily through tapping into her sad feelings; with Tom, by stirring emotions from his childhood but primarily through education—and being aware of and meeting their expectations even to a small degree. The process, not the content, is your template.

This went well for both of them, but in the next chapter we'll talk about the challenges—situations in which the process goes less smoothly.

CHAPTER 4

First-Session First Aid

IN THE IDEAL WORLD all your first sessions run smoothly. You feel satisfied that you've accomplished your goals, and your client is eager to come back and get to work. But in the real world, it can be bumpier. Emotions, time, unexpected twists and turns threaten to drive everything off course; clients leave ambivalent or unsettled. In this chapter we'll map out the most common trouble spots you're likely to encounter. We'll take them one by one, describing the problem, the dynamics, and possible solutions.

Trouble Spot #1: The Resistant Client

Most clients come voluntarily. Perhaps they have been in therapy before and found it helpful, or they are looking for other options to handle an internal or relationship problem that has been driving them crazy; they come to see what you and your therapy have to offer. As we've been saying all along, this is what makes the first session important: It is your opportunity to help clients understand and experience you and your therapy in the best light so they can make a clear and honest decision whether this is or is not a good means to their end.

But some clients come with a different attitude. Take Jack. He shows up in your office because the Department of Social Services said in its protective order that he was abusive and needs to seek counseling. He lost it one day, exploding on his 8-year-old son one morning last week, pushing and slapping him. He was busted when the teachers noticed the marks on his child's arms and the side of his face. Jack doesn't want to be there and tells you exactly that.

Sources of Resistance

Much has been written about resistance in therapy. From the psychodynamic perspective, it is pretty much assumed that it is always part and parcel of the clinical process, and much of this longer-term work focuses on slowly dismantling it. If we look at resistance from a practical perspective, there are four common and interrelated sources of resistance (Taibbi, 2007):

No Agreement about the Problem. This can come in two forms. The first is that there is no problem. A judge orders a defendant to go to anger management after she appears in court for domestic violence. The defendant sees her actions as an isolated incident, a flare-up fueled only by alcohol, and there is no underlying anger issue to address. Or even though the judge doesn't seem to believe her, she thinks that her actions were only in self-defense, in response to her partner cussing her out and wagging his finger in her face. Or a mother drags in her teen because the mother thinks her son has a marijuana addiction. He says he only smokes a little and that everyone at school does the same or worse. The resistance here comes because the client feels there is nothing to fix. It's actually the judge or the partner or the mother who has the problem.

The other form is that you and client don't agree on the problem. This is where Tom, your client from the last chapter, voices worry about his anger, but can't make the connection when you tie his anger to underlying anxiety and hyper-vigilance. You pitch your treatment plan on this focus, but he isn't buying it.

Poor Pacing. Pacing in therapy is exactly what the word means: going either too fast or too slow. *Too slow* is the three-session assessment for the client who is expecting recommen-dations by the end of the first. *Too fast* is doing an experiential exercise at the top of the first session, or assigning homework that is too emotionally difficult ("So, why don't you give your father—to whom you haven't spoken in 20 years—a call some-time this week?"). One client drops out after two sessions of assessment, another doesn't return after the experiential exer-cise, and the third says he didn't have time to call his father.

Faulty Expectations of the Process. In some ways, poor pacing is a subset of faulty expectations—for example, the cli-ent not expecting that three-session assessment—but it can be broader than that. The mother thought that you would see the pot-smoking son by himself, rather than with her, and give him a clinical talking-to that would straighten him up. Tom wants techniques to manage his anger, but you drill down into his childhood session after session. The couple thought you would declare once and for all who was right (sane) and who was wrong (crazy). Or, more simply, the client thought that his insurance covered the entire cost and that there was no copay.

Old Wounds Get Triggered. You ask Ellen why she didn't follow through with her homework and call her sister this past week, and she hears in your question and voice her scolding father; she emotionally turns into a 6-year-old, gets quiet, and stares at her shoes. Or, you offhandedly and lightly touch your client, who has a history of sexual abuse, on the shoulder on the way out of your office, and she freezes and cancels her next appointment. Or a client in crisis leaves a long emotional voice message on your phone, but the phone service is down and you don't get the message until the next day; she feels abandoned and unimportant, and never returns your call. Old emotional wounds are triggered, making the therapeutic relationship and therapy process feel unsafe.

Although client resistance comes in a variety of forms—canceling or dropping out, not doing the assignments, arguing back or shutting down—regardless of the source, what you see as resistance is, for the client, a bad solution to another problem, a problem that always begins with you.

Countering Resistance

We're back to leadership: to tracking the process like a bloodhound to be sure that you and the client are in lockstep, to clearly defining the problem and the expectations as quickly as possible, and to anticipating transferences. And when you sense the relationship moving out of lockstep and suspect that an old wound has just been triggered, you move quickly to repair: "Was calling your father too difficult?" "Did my touching of your shoulder feel threatening in some way?"—all said in a gentle tone.

Your sensitivity to these bumps in the clinical process and your asking the hard questions and fixing the relationship by fixing your clinical mistakes are the antidote to most issues of resistance. But what about those situations such as Jack's, who comes in with guns blazing at the start, where there is no relationship, no process to correct? You ask him why he doesn't want to be here with you, and he goes on to explain why he felt he really didn't do anything that wrong. He starts a rant about the way parents can't raise their own children anymore, that everyone's got their nose in everyone else's business, that if that were his father and he said what his son had said to him, he'd have a lot more than just a couple of marks on his arm, believe you me. He's clearly in the category of clients who don't agree that there is a problem—or, in his words, the only problem is other people telling him how to raise his kids.

You let him talk and when he finally begins to run out of steam, you say that he's right, that when he was growing up Social Services and the courts didn't get involved with parenting or focus on abuse as much. But times have changed, and the reality is that now we think differently about the community's responsibility to children, and that many children do, in fact, become dangerously abused. If his dad were raising him today, his dad would likely be sitting in that same chair, and perhaps some of the pain that he as a child may have experienced might have been prevented.

This may or may not impress him. In these openly resistant situations where clients are only there because someone is making them—a parent, the courts, an attorney—they may, at best, go through the motions to get through the process. Handling this as you would any client objection, you want to avoid pushing too hard and potentially creating a power struggle with the client. Therapy is a service, and service and enforcement do not mix. It's also all too easy in cases like this to blur means and ends and ultimately lose sight of the ends. Jack comes in fighting therapy, missing the real point that he can't abuse his son when he gets angry. Therapy is one means to help him do that: to learn to manage his anger better, to learn other ways of disciplining (not *not* disciplining, as he believes) his children. He can even bring in his son and you both can work to together to try and "straighten him out," or bring in the entire rest of the family and get his wife onboard as well.

So you present him with a clear picture of what therapy can and cannot do, you correct any distortions in expectations he probably has in his head, and you convey empathy and avoid sounding like an enforcer. You might ask him if he is willing to try this for three sessions and see if he changes his mind. And, you emphasize that it is about the bottom line: that he needs to find a way to *not* repeat his behavior. If he has another idea—that he wants to talk to his minister instead of you, or is willing to attend a parenting class or get a consult for medication—he should go talk to his attorney and see if that option is acceptable. But, you say, if he doesn't want to come back, that's up to him; you don't want him to waste your or his time. You'll be happy to write a letter saying that he did come in and that you are agreeing that continuing at this point would not be clinically productive. The best you can do is, once again, the best you can do.

Trouble Spot #2: The Ambivalent Client

Whereas resistant clients know they don't want to be there, ambivalent clients aren't sure. They usually break down into two different camps: Those who are ambivalent about therapy itself and those who are ambivalent about you or your approach. Let's look at these one at a time.

Ambivalence about Therapy

Those who are ambivalent about therapy generally have never been in therapy, or perhaps had an awful one-session experience that left them gun-shy about the entire process. Behind the ambivalence are questions sometimes clearly voiced, other times less so. Clients may wonder if therapy can actually help with their problem—"How can talking to a stranger about something I've been dealing with for a long time actually make things better?"—or whether they actually need it—"I'm not sure it's that bad that I can't handle it on my own"—and avoid taking this next step.

Of course, the commitment of time or money is readily a concern for many, especially when tainted by their own impressions or the stories of others that they are entering a process that is long and difficult to disengage from once started, or that necessarily leads to things getting worse before they get better. Finally, they may worry about being judged: that they may hear from you that they and their problems are actually much worse than they themselves thought, and that it's clearly their fault.

Sometimes the ambivalence is apparent in that initial pre-session contact. You return Jamal's phone call and ask if he'd like to schedule an appointment and you hear that wobbly "I guess." At this point you may take to a few minutes to explore: "Hmm, you sound a bit hesitant. Do you have any questions that I could answer for you?" You see if you can uncover the source of Jamal's caution.

Other times the potential client will ask the questions directly: "I've never done therapy before. Can you tell me more about how this may help me with my anxiety?" Or, "I went to see this woman a few months ago, and she was just weird, and I never went back. I don't want to have an experience like that again." Or, "My girlfriend thinks I have a problem with drinking. Sometimes I think she might be right, but most of the time I think it's just because I have a lot of stress right now on my job. I'm wondering if I should just see what happens with the job." Or, "My insurance has a cap on sessions and I don't want to be in a situation where I start but then wind up footing a huge bill out of my pocket."

You can think of these questions and comments as initial client objections and handle them as such. You explain how your approach to therapy can help the client's anxiety. You ask what was weird about the client's past experience and explain how your approach is different. You say, yes, stress and drinking often go hand in hand; if he is willing to come in for an initial consult, you can give him some idea of the ways therapy could help him better handle his stress and explore further whether there may be a deeper alcohol problem. You say that although you're not immediately familiar with the client's insurance, you tend to do short-term therapy, and if there is a need to continue beyond the capped sessions, that you can both discuss some payment options. You provide the information the client needs to relieve his anxiety and help him make a decision.

Of course, ambivalence can also be apparent at the start of the first session. In your opening with Tonya, she says that she has never been in therapy before. When you ask what you can help her with, she says that she's always had a problem with depression, she guesses, but has always managed to "get along." But when her brother visited last week and asked how she was doing, she talked about feeling down and not sleeping well. He mentioned that he had gone to see a counselor last year when he was struggling after his divorce and found it really helpful, and encouraged her to do the same. So, she says, she's here to see what this is like.

The advantage you obviously have at this point is that she is indeed here, and you have the entire session to help her decide as you move through the goals, track the process, build rapport, and help her feel safe. Your treatment plan will address her depression, and you'll help her see how your form of therapy can help her actually feel better and not just "get along." And, most importantly, before the end the session, you are going to return to the beginning: "At the beginning of the session you sounded unsure about how you felt about therapy. How did this go for you today? Was it helpful? Do you think you would like to continue?"

And then, as always, you listen for what she says next: "Yes, actually this is really helpful and not as scary as I imagined. I'd like to come back." *(Good to go.)* Or, "This was good. Let me think about it." *(Hmmm . . .)* "That's fine," you say. "Are there any other questions that I can answer for you?" She may truly need time to process and decide, or she may raise a question that you haven't covered—payments, schedule— or she says that she has the name of another therapist that she was thinking of calling as well. Again, your response is, "That's fine. I appreciate your coming in today. Let me know if there are any other questions or information that you need."

Ambivalence about You or Your Therapeutic Approach
Just as ambivalence about therapy stems from unanswered questions and anxiety, so too does clients' ambivalence about you and your approach. Tonya's "think about it" statement may reflect some lingering issues about therapy itself, but also after the session hour, about you and what you can offer. By doing comparative shopping, she will hopefully be able to answer her questions and make a decision.

Many of those who have been in therapy before come away from those experiences with a better sense of what they *don't* want than what they do want to focus on in treatment: "I've been in therapy many times before, and am tired of talking about my childhood"; "I've seen a solution-focused, short-term therapist before, but feel that it didn't get to the core of my issues"; "The last therapist I saw for a few sessions seemed to be constantly pushing medication, which I was clear I was uncomfortable with." The stated or implied next sentence is: "Is your approach more of the same or different?" And you answer honestly and explain your rationale for your approach.

For others there are concerns about gender or style: "I've seen women therapists in the past, but my friend highly recommended you; frankly I'm a bit nervous talking to a man." Or, "I liked my last therapist a lot, but she also talked a lot about herself rather than me." Or, "My last therapist was a nice guy, but he didn't offer any concrete advice in the session." Gender is often a make-or-break issue for many clients; the transference issues are simply too overwhelming, and the best you can offer is to meet with them for one session and see how it goes. For the others who have misgivings about their past therapists, you point out differences of your own approach.

And if your approach does indeed happen to be similar to those of past therapists—that you too tend to be less directive or behavioral—explain your rationale behind it and explain how you feel your approach can still be effective in treating their presenting problems. That is, use information to change the emotional climate: "I think in terms of attachment and in my way of thinking about your problem, I would focus on . . . "; "I choose this approach because research has shown that. . . . "

Finally, make sure you circle back to the client's initial concerns by the end of the session: "So, you had mixed feelings about seeing a male therapist. How was this for you today?

Did it feel okay, or did it still feel awkward?" And again you see what the client says next and counter the objections.

Trouble Spot #3: The Client in Crisis

You've undoubtedly been in a state of crisis at some point in the past. You suddenly experienced severe pain. Your car broke down in the middle of the interstate. The school called and said that you needed to come to the principal's office right away because your kid is in trouble. Your toilet won't flush and 10 people are coming over for dinner in an hour.

What you probably wanted most at those times was immediate action—a doctor to diagnose and treat your pain, a tow-truck to show up and handle your car, information about what has happened at school, a plumber who can come over in 15 minutes and unclog the toilet. Psychological problems are no different. A woman calls and leaves a rushed message saying that she had a terrible fight with her husband that morning, is thinking of leaving him, and needs to see someone right away. A mother leaves a message that she just had a meeting with the guidance counselor at school and she left feeling overwhelmed and worried about her son's acting out. A man leaves a message that simply says, "I need to see you as soon as possible."

Responding to a crisis is about putting out, as quickly as possible, the emotional fire the client feels; this is your primary focus from that first contact through your first session with any client in crisis. Depending on how the first session unfolds—on how much time and effort it may take to change the emotional climate and lower the client's anxiety—you may need to sacrifice your other first-session goals of discerning expectations, assessment, and even precise treatment planning in the process.

You call the client in crisis back and, leaving yourself enough time, allow the client to vent: The woman describes the fight, the mother relates what the school counselor said, the man explains that he believes he has been having mild but frequent anxiety attacks in the past week. You listen empathically and actively, and use your clinical judgment to map out next steps: "There is a shelter here in town for women and children," you say to the woman, "and here is the number"; "I have a cancellation for 4:00 this afternoon and can see you and your son then"; "I can see you first thing tomorrow morning," you say to the gentleman, "but in the meantime if you become more concerned or your anxiety worsens, contact your family doctor or go to the emergency room." And if you can't see them—you have no openings, or you will be out of town for the next 2 weeks—give them names and numbers of other therapists, the number for the community mental health center, and so on—give them *something*, rather than just saying sorry.

Providing next steps and options to these clients is essential. There is a vast emotional difference between the tow-truck operator who doesn't return your call and the one who says that he can be there within an hour but in the meantime call *77 to contact the Highway Patrol. Individuals in crisis have tunnel vision, and your leadership and suggestions not only convey your concern, but also provide them with an action plan at a time when they are not sure what action to take—which is extremely helpful in reducing their anxiety.

Some crises, however, may turn out to be not true crises after all. John calls you and says that he was given your name by his attorney. He explains that he's got himself in a bind, is scheduled to appear in court in 2 days, and is wondering if he can see you today or tomorrow. He explains that his attorney suggested getting a note from you that he can present to the judge saying that he did indeed come in to see you and is about to start therapy.

Although John may be in some state of urgency, even anxiety, is this a true crisis? There's a manipulative quality here; you sense going-through-the-motions behavior. Why is he putting this off to the last minute, you wonder? John seems to be seeking you out because his attorney suggested it, not because he is highly concerned about his own behavior or problems. So you listen, ask questions, and make your own clinical judgment: Does John truly have some clinical goals? If you can't see him until next week, is he still interested in coming in? Some clinicians will go ahead and schedule the appointment quickly if they can and assess the need and goals once the client is in session. Others, feeling manipulated, may say that they don't, in fact, have time, but that John is free to call back after he sees what happens in court. Your call.

Trouble Spot #4: The Emotional Breakdown

Closely linked to clients in crisis are those who emotionally break down during the first session. Sometimes the cause is situational. Terry schedules an appointment to meet with you about job issues, but in the first session she comes in looking shaken. When you ask if she is all right, she says that she is upset because she just received a call from her sister-in-law that her brother was in a car accident that morning and is now in the hospital. She hasn't heard anything about his condition. She then begins to tear up.

Other clients break down simply because they are flooded

with emotion. Henry, a fireman, starts talking about an alarm that his crew answered last week, and as he begins to describe his efforts to save the children inside the house, he falls apart, sobbing. Clare begins to describe her struggle with her critical supervisor, then suddenly shifts gears and launches into an angry tirade about how her supervisor is just like her father who also always criticized her—nothing she could do was right!

This level of intensity can be unnerving in a first session, especially when you had no clue that the client was in such a state. Once again, your focus is on putting out the emotional fire. You remain calm. What is unfolding at this point has little to do with you, rapport, or trust, but about someone reaching his or her emotional limit. You actively listen, you let the client vent, you don't interrupt. You resist the urge to fix or drill down into content. You're tracking the process.

And you're also watching the clock. Thank God, you think, this isn't happening at the end of the hour, but as we discussed earlier, enduring 50 minutes of ranting or sobbing is never a good idea because you're left with no time to help the client emotionally settle. So you watch to see whether Henry is slowing down; you track to make sure that Clare is not spiraling up even more, and you're careful not to fuel her emotional fire by asking her to give you other examples of her father's hurtful behavior.

But if Henry is not settling down or Clare is indeed becoming more agitated as time is running out, you need to put on the emotional brakes. How do you do this? You pull them back to the here and now: You ask them to make eye contact, to take a few deep breaths. You help shut down their emotional amygdala by activating their rational prefrontal lobes: "So, what did your captain say after the fire was put out?"

"Tell me what you said to your supervisor when she criticized your work last week." You talk about the process and bring them back in the room: "I know, this is difficult, but I don't want you to leave here upset. Tell me what you had planned for the rest of today." Again, this is leadership, this is tracking the process, this is changing the emotional climate.

Trouble Spot #5: The Silent or Inhibited Client

If the emotional breakdown can be unnerving because of so much stimulation, the inhibited or silent client can be unnerving because of the lack of it. There's nothing to grasp onto, or the process plods along in slow-motion and you're worried about running out of time with not much said, let alone goals accomplished. This is a case of determining the problem under the problem: the possible reason for the silence or inhibited conversation. Here are the common sources:

Angry Silence

The 17-year-old is told to go to counseling and is dropped off by the parents; the husband's wife threatens divorce if he doesn't get help for his constant irritability. The 17-year-old feels like she has no voice or choice, and the husband is showing up solely to get his wife off his back. These are resistant clients who don't want to be there; someone else sees a problem that they don't, or they may even agree there is some small problem but certainly don't believe that therapy is the way to solve it.

You give words to the anger—that you could imagine that the teen's angry because her parents said she had to come; that the husband maybe feels that he doesn't have a problem or that maybe he does get irritable, but she is the one who. . . .

You sound calm and gentle so you don't replicate the pressure or criticism and spark transference reactions. You talk about therapy as a service, about helping people solve problems, and even if she or he doesn't agree with what others are saying is a problem, is there something to fix? Would it be helpful, you say to the teen, to have your parents come in and find out what they are so upset about? What about having your wife come in, you say to the husband, so he can help her understand his side of the story?

The goal here is simply changing the process—communicating about emotions rather than stonewalling, finding ways to help the clients open up. And when they do, you stay quiet, listen and respond empathically—becoming the ideal parent, the ideal partner—to make it as easy as possible for them to continue. Your goal—to have them relax and see if, by the end of the hour, you both can agree on a problem important for them to focus upon—however vague or even unreasonable it may seem on the surface—so that they are willing to come back.

Anxious Silence

Those who tend to be anxious are usually not so much silent as hesitant. They may be struggling with generalized or social anxiety, and the simple fact of meeting a new person and having a conversation is difficult. They may worry about being judged and so they deliberate about what and what not to say; or being a bit perfectionistic, they may worry that what they are saying is exactly right; or they talk in a vague, intellectual, amorphous way that makes it difficult for you to get a handle on exactly what it is they are struggling with and want to fix.

Your goal, once again, is to lower their anxiety. Just as you say what the angry client may be thinking, you can do the same here—"Take your time, there is no need to rush"; "Start wherever you like"; "There is no right answer"—and you sound gentle and calm. Because questions raise anxiety, make statements: Rather than, "Why did you say that?" say instead, "I'm wondering why you said that." Give compliments along the way: "You're did a great job describing that. What I'm confused about is. . . . " Again, track the process. Notice their breathing. The goal is to increase communication, help them feel safe. Content is not important right now. Be the ideal parent to help them settle.

Depressed Silence

For severely depressed clients, it is not about the interaction with you but about the interaction between them and the stuff in their heads. Although anxiety and depression often go together, the more anxious clients will be looking at you, trying to read cues. The depressed clients are more likely looking down or off into space, absorbed in their own thoughts and ruminations.

Because depressed clients are struggling so hard with their own thoughts, you need to keep your questions and comments simple. Again, talk quietly and calmly, matching their presentation, and make questions that require only yes-or-no-type responses. Rather than asking, "What medications are you currently taking?" instead ask, "Are you taking medication for your depression?" If yes, ask about common types—Prozac? Lexapro? Zoloft? If the client seems befuddled in his storytelling or is struggling to stay on track—"I forgot what I was talking about"—help him out—"You mentioned seeing your sister"—or talk about the process—"Do my questions seem hard to answer?"; "Would it help us to get started if I asked some questions first?" As always, what you are trying to do is move into lockstep with the client, through trial and error discovering what pace and what phrasing make it easiest for the client to convey his thoughts.

The Intellectually Impaired Client

Just as you want to simplify questions and statements with clients overwhelmed by depression, so too do you want to do the same with clients who are intellectually impaired. Keep questions to simple yes-and-no answers. Ask one question at a time and ask leading questions: "Did you feel angry?" Focus on concrete behaviors—"What did you do?"—rather than "Why did you do that?" Often it is helpful to have a friend or family member join the session both to help the client feel safer and because he or she is familiar with the client's comprehension level and is able to "translate" your questions and comments.

Where you may sometimes become frustrated or confused is when you are working with clients whose intellectual impairment is minor—those with a borderline IQ, for example. Let's say that you spend the first session with Susan talking about problems with getting her children to behave. She seems to be engaged throughout the session and in-step with you when you present your treatment plan and suggest to her that she develop a reward chart to encourage more positive behaviors in her children. But when she returns the following week, you find out that she didn't do the homework you had suggested, seems passive, and lacks an agenda. You feel like you are starting all over.

It's easy for you to interpret Susan's response as some form of passive resistance, but it isn't. The problem is that although you thought you were both staying in lockstep, you weren't. Like many with such intellectual impairments, in the process of learning to socially adapt with her disability, Susan knew to watch your cues and knew how to seem engaged when in actuality she didn't fully understand everything you were presenting. The reward chart didn't get completed because she didn't fully understand the instructions, or the process itself seemed too complicated to carry out.

Susan's "not-doing" was her solution to an underlying problem, in this case, to your plan and assignment seeming too overwhelming or difficult. Follow up, break it down. Isolate the underlying problem: "I'm wondering why you didn't try the reward chart. Was my description hard to understand? Would it be helpful if we made one together right now?"

Trouble Spot #6: The Unexpected Objection

You actually think you did a good job in this first session, closely tracking the process, changing the emotional climate, and facilitating your client's acceptance of your treatment plan. But then as you're wrapping up, she presents an objection that surprises you. Following the guidelines discussed in Chapter 2, here are some of the common objections and ways to respond:

- *"I'm not sure how I feel about this approach."* You respond: "That's fine, I understand. It's natural to feel a bit uncertain at first since this is new and something you have not done before. But most people *(consensus)* find that it is not as difficult as they imagined and they find this approach to be really helpful." Or: "I'm wondering if there is something specific that is bothering you about what I've suggested. Is there something that you are particularly uncomfortable with?"
- *"Let me think about it"* or *"Let me check my work schedule."*

You respond: "That's fine. Is there anything else you need to know? You seem hesitant, and I'm just wondering why." Or: "That's fine. If you have any more questions, please give me a call. I really think that we can work together and fix this problem. Or I'd be happy to check back with you in the next few days."

- *"Let me talk to my partner <or whomever>."* You respond: "That's fine. I'd be happy to talk to her as well if she has any questions; she can simply give me a call. Just so I can make sure I have time if you decide to come back in, especially since you need a later appointment *(scarcity)*, I'm wondering if it might be a good idea to pencil something in and then you can let me know in the next day or so." Or coach the client on what to say to the partner (or whomever): "That's fine. If you talk to your partner, I would suggest that you ask if she is willing to come in with you one time. Say she doesn't have to talk, but this is more a forum for her to just listen to you so that you can help her better understand how you feel."

The thinking behind this cautionary comment about not having to talk is that family members are often reluctant to come in because they fear being put on the spot and having to defend themselves, being pressured to talk about topics that they don't want to talk about, or getting pulled into ongoing therapy. Telling them that they need to come in only the one time and are not expected to unpack their inner psyche helps them relax and be more open. It is your job to engage such visitors and help them decide what role they want to play, if any, in your client's treatment.

If you have built rapport and done a good job of tracking the process, these last-minute objections should be rare. That said, don't kick yourself if they occasionally arise. What you are doing in managing these end-of-session surprises is *not* to awkwardly try to rally a last-minute defense of yourself or your treatment plan and approach, but rather to end the session on an emotional note that leaves the client feeling heard and keeps open the option of further sessions.

Following Up

Throughout this chapter we have been talking about ways to manage those clients and situations that have the potential to throw you off course and derail your standard first-session itinerary. But sometimes, even with your best efforts to track the process, change the emotional climate, and end on a good note, you don't. You somehow do run out of time. The client gets upset and abruptly walks out in the middle of the session or is still emotionally upset by the end. What do you do next?

You follow up. The easiest way to do this is to call. Depending on your own concern and the emotional state of the client, you can call within an hour to the next day. (Obviously, if you felt this was a psychological emergency—the client was potentially suicidal or homicidal—you would take proper legal action such as notifying police.) Although you want to give the client an opportunity to emotionally settle on her own, you don't want to put off your check-in call for days. Long delays may make your message seem like an afterthought and that your voiced concern isn't really a concern.

Your goal with such follow-ups is to check in on the client emotionally and repair the relationship. If you get the client's voicemail, leave a message saying what you noticed and what the client might be thinking and feeling:

"John, I realized that you were upset when you left this morning. I'm just calling to check in with you and see how you are doing. I'd be happy to talk with you on the phone. Feel free to give me a call."

Or:

"John, I'm just calling to check in on you. I didn't mean to get you upset by asking about your mom, and I'm sorry we didn't have more time to talk about it further. I'd like to know how you are doing. Feel free to give me a call."

At that point John may call back and leave a message saying that he is okay, or that he does want to talk and leaves you some good times to call back.

Suppose you actually reach John on the phone instead of reaching his voicemail. Such a call often catches clients off course—they may be at work or driving—and it isn't a good time to talk. Again, you say what you think the client may be thinking:

"Hi, John. I was just calling to check on you. I know you left here feeling upset. I just wanted to know if you're okay. I realize I might be putting you on the spot and that this is not a good time to talk."

John may say yes, he is doing okay, and no, this isn't a good time to talk, but that he will give you a call later—or that actually this is an okay time to talk.

You should assume that clients may be able to talk with you and so you want to call when you have at least a few minutes to talk with them. If after a few minutes John still has more to say, be courteous, apologize and say that you need to stop, and that you'd be happy to call back later at an agreed time. If John sounds like he is in a good place emotionally, suggest that you could talk about this further at the next appointment. Again, the goal here is conveying concern—that the client left unsettled, may be upset with you, and that you want to help repair the misunderstanding and relationship.

And if the client doesn't call back? Leave two more messages—any more can border on stalking. Say in the last that you're assuming that the client is okay but has decided not to continue now. Say that the door is always open for the client to come back, and if, for whatever reason, the client would like a referral to someone else, that he should feel free to leave you a message. Some clinicians send a certified letter to clients saying the same as way of documenting the termination of the clinical relationship so that there is no danger of the client perceiving abandonment. The psychological aim here, as mentioned earlier, is to reduce any awkwardness or guilt that the client may have about the ending, and which may interfere with returning at a later time.

First Aid for First Sessions

We've been discussing those clients and session processes where you can get derailed. But even with long-standing clients—those clients who are deeply invested in the clinical relationship—there are bumps in the therapeutic road where topics trigger strong emotional reactions, where your process ignites transference reactions that you constantly need to be alert to and repair. When seeing a client the first time, you are, understandably, blind to much of this. You can only make semi-informed guesses and clinical decisions based on your clinical experience and cues gathered on the fly throughout the session.

Because therapy is a pragmatic sport, not a cut-and-dry endeavor like plumbing or computer repair, you do your best, realize that there is much outside your control but that through your own reflection and clinical supervision, you can learn from such experiences.

Over time, your best will become ever better.

CHAPTER 5

First Sessions with Couples

Hᴏᴘᴇғᴜʟʟʏ, ʏᴏᴜ ɴᴏᴡ ʜᴀᴠᴇ a foundation for successfully conducting your first sessions with individual clients and know how to tackle those trouble spots that can derail you. In this chapter we move to new territory: work with couples. In this chapter we'll discuss the challenges that couples can present to both the content and process of the first session and describe concrete ways to successfully shape the couple session.

The Unique Landscape of Couple Work

While the core skills are the same, in many ways couple work is more difficult than individual work for a number of reasons, primarily centering around the 3-person triangle always in the room. In this section we'll map out the terrain of couple work and contrast it with that of individuals.

Balance

When it's just you and the client together in the room, your undistracted focus helps to ensure that you stay in lockstep. With an individual, changing the emotional climate, moving

into deeper topics, and creating the intimacy that is character-
istic of individual therapy can all happen quickly.

Not so with couples. There's a two-pronged focus in place,
and more importantly, that troublesome triangle in the room
means that there are two in, one out . . . *always*. Your challenge throughout the session is to jockey from one to the
other and sometimes to both, supporting one partner when
you need to without alienating the other, talking directly to
the couple as a unit with the hope that both partners hear and
take away the same message. Tricky stuff.

One good way of negotiating a path through this quagmire
is to stay especially focused on process rather than getting lost
in the content, which is now doubled, of each partner's story.
Focus less on individual personalities and pathologies; side-
step the pull to either arbitrate or advocate for each individual's view of reality by sifting through content. Instead focus
more on the interactional patterns unfolding in the room: the
way each partner emotionally and behaviorally acts and reacts
to the other, forming set sequences. These unfolding dysfunc-
tional patterns are the problem in motion. By stopping these
patterns, and then helping the partners become aware of and
change them, you and they are dismantling the obstacles to
connection and problem solving right there and then.

We'll illustrate more of these ideas later in the chapter.
The point to remember now is that maintaining balance is
the key. All the other challenges of couple work derive from
this one.

Leadership

As we've been discussing all along, strong leadership is always
an essential element of any first session. But in order to manage the flow of conversation, stop and change interactional

patterns, and ensure that balance is achieved throughout the session, you need to keep a firmer grasp on the conversational reins. And because many couples arrive in crisis—the big fight over the weekend that resulted in the police being called, the stomping out of one partner who spent the last few days with parents—and may begin the session with residual anger and anxiety, or simply are able to easily push each other's emotional buttons, it doesn't take much for emotions to quickly gather momentum and spin out of control. Within nanoseconds the couple is arguing about Christmas 2010 again or someone's mother, or one partner is emotionally breaking down and sobbing within minutes of telling her story.

Although you want to be ready to step in when this happens, you don't need to maintain the hypervigilance of an attack dog. When the conversation begins to go off the rails, wait a minute or two and see if the individuals themselves can rein in the emotion, get back on track, slow the escalation: "Hold on," says John, "I don't want to go down that road of Christmas again. What I'm trying to say, Lindsey, is . . . "; or Jessie begins to cry but then pulls herself together and allows her husband David to speak.

If they can't—John and Lindsey escalate, Jessie's sobs become stronger—you do need to take action. You can ask the partners to take turns speaking without any interruption by the other, or you can ask each of them to talk to you rather than the partner, with you shaping the conversation via your questions and comments. You can help Jessie emotionally settle, for example, by asking questions that tap into her rational, rather than emotional, brain: "What is your explanation for this?" rather than "Tell me what is making you so upset." Or you can shift the tone by shifting the topic: "I understand that that was a difficult time, but can you tell me about good times in your relationship?" rather than unintentionally feeding the emotional fire by remaining silently empathic.

And if that fails—Lindsey continues to make provoking comments while John is speaking, or they fall back into escalation and you can't contain them; Jessie remains overwrought and inconsolable—you need to separate the partners: "John, would you mind going out to the waiting room while I talk with Lindsay? Give us about 10 minutes, and then I'll talk with you"; "David, could you give me and Jessie a few minutes alone and then you and I can talk?"

Once separated, use the individual time to calm the clients by allowing them to vent their emotions and pinpoint what is upsetting them so much. Create balance by making sure you leave time to see the partners and hear their side of the story. And if you have a few minutes to see them together at the end of the session, do so. Explain the next steps to them: that you will see them together next time, that you want to clarify mutual treatment goals, and so on.

As we mentioned in the last chapter about handling trouble spots, taking the step of separating the partners and using the session time to perform emotional first aid likely aborts your own first-session agenda. But you are making a sound clinical decision—namely, setting as a priority a change in the interactional process and emotional climate in a way that maintains balance. If you don't—if you let John and Lindsey, for example, continue to escalate in the session—you are, by your inaction, inadvertently condoning their destructive behaviors. Rather than feeling safe, they will feel unsafe; they will see you as ineffective and realize that they just spent money doing in your office what they could have done at home for free.

Similarly, if you let Jessie dominate the session with her

tears, believing, perhaps, that such catharsis is an opportunity for the couple to reach some emotional breakthrough, Jessie may at best feel supported, but David is likely to go away feeling that you deliberately took her side, that you have been "sucked" into her drama, and that you are not interested in what he has to say. No good can come from such inaction. They are likely not to return.

Watching the Clock

When working with individuals, you watch the clock to make sure there is enough time to accomplish what needs to be accomplished in the session. With couples the need is the same, but with the added dimension, once again, of maintaining balance. You can think of yourself not as just a session timekeeper with couples, but more like an NFL referee who is not just tracking the game clock, but also is vigilant about time spent in huddles, on the line, and in time-outs. Because you are sorting out two stories, not just one, you need to make sure, particularly in the opening segment of the session, that both partners are heard and have a chance to present their concerns so that you get a more rounded picture of the problem and both partners can leave feeling heard. Again, you can't afford to allow Jessie to sob for 40 minutes, for John and Lindsey to continue to rant.

Building Rapport

Because you are focusing on two different individuals, you are challenged to connect with both. To do this, you need to assess the needs of each for creating safety. Here you look at potentially differing sensory language—visual, auditory, kinesthetic. You need to mirror different body positions, adjust your voice tone and language for each—using coarser language with Bill perhaps or mirroring Angie's quiet speech—focusing on different topics in order to build connections—asking more about Bill's interest in motorcycles or the college courses that Angie is taking. This isn't clinically difficult, but it does require your being attentive and intentional to each of the individuals.

Transference

You face the same split-focus balancing act regarding transference as you do with rapport building. You're looking for transference cues throughout the session—for example, Alan's struggle with confrontation, Kim's flaring up over criticism. What makes couple work a bit easier in this regard is that many couples inadvertently and automatically trigger each other's emotional wounds and their concomitant transference reactions in the session process. You'll likely to see, for example, Alan hesitate or withdraw rather than challenge Kim, or notice Kim emotionally spiraling over a relatively bland comment by Alan. Marking these over- and underreactions in the session helps you discern these emotional sensitivities and then counter them by adapting an ideal-parent, counterpoint position: "Alan," you say gently, "you seem tentative"; "Kim," you say quietly, "what just hurt your feelings?"

Emotional Climate

The escalating couple and the emotionally overwhelmed client create, as mentioned, obvious situations in which you particularly need to work hard to change the climate in the room. But for the less emotional couple, the need to change the climate, just as you do with individuals, still remains, but again with balance as a priority. The tools and techniques for doing so described earlier apply here as well: use of the ideal scenario or perspective, for example, shifting to soft emotions, and particularly in the case of couples, shifting to positive emotions by talking about what is good in the relationship rather than what is a problem.

Another climate-changing tool that is particularly effective with couples is education, specifically providing information about normal adult and relationship development, the basics of communication skills, the 7-year itch, the impact of childhood emotional wounds on relationships. What you choose will obviously reflect your own clinical orientation. The reason education can have such a strong impact is that most couples come in either in a swirl of overwhelming content and have difficulty seeing a larger, different perspective, or they come in embarrassed and ashamed that their relationship has reached the state that they have to turn to outside professional help.

Through education and your expert role you have the opportunity to reframe their perspectives and concerns. By explaining that their problems and concerns are, in fact, not unusual but common, not the result of defective character but a matter of learning new skills, that they are extremely healthy simply because they are willing to seek outside help and approach their problems head-on, you assuage the partners' anxiety and shame by normalizing their feelings. Just as you want to mentally have treatment plans in place for a range of presenting problems, it's useful to have educational frames at the ready to present (see Gottman, 2000; Hendrix, 2007; Taibbi, 2007). Having them at the ready keeps you from scrambling to create one for similar couples.

Expectations

As with individuals, each partner comes to the first session with some expectation about the process, based upon previous experience, stories from friends, television shows and movies. Here again part of the first-session agenda is uncovering and bringing these expectations in line with your own approach. While we would like to think that partners who are struggling with their relationship sit down at some point, acknowledge and agree not only on the nature of their difficulties, but also on what they want to most get out of it to put their problems to rest, a majority of them find the path to your door through a less "reasonable" route.

Here are some of the common expectations that are unique to couple work:

The Drop-Off. William Doherty (2013) notes that there is always someone who is "in" in terms of being motivated for couple therapy and repairing the relationship, and someone who is "out"—that is, more ambivalent about the clinical process and the relationship. Your challenge in terms of balance is bringing this "out" person in. The drop-off is where this being "out" comes to the fore, and there are several variations of it.

I remember seeing a couple early in my career wherein the husband had called to schedule the appointment. When he and his wife arrived, he immediately launched into a somewhat prepared speech, which, because I was young, inexperienced, and somewhat intimidated, did nothing to halt. What he essentially said to his wife was that he was in fact gay, had realized it many years ago, but now felt he needed to stop living a secret life. He was planning on moving out later in the week and moving in with his lover. His wife started to cry. I was speechless.

Before I could gather my wits about me, he was gone—literally. He "just realized" that he was late for an important meeting at work, needed to leave, and sprinted out the door. There his wife and I sat.

This is the ultimate drop-off. The husband had arranged to secure a safe place to make his announcement and then leave both the therapy and the relationship, with me to mop up. For some others the drop-off involves a partner who has already decided to separate or divorce—much like my case—has no interest in doing therapy, and perhaps goes through the motions of attending a few sessions, feigns interest, does little or no homework, and then drops out. The agenda here is to be able to say to the partner, and perhaps to himself, that he tried therapy before deciding it was time to move on.

In more common cases, one partner essentially believes that all the problems lie in the personality of the other, and much of the session is about making a case for why the focus needs to be on individual therapy for that partner, rather than couple therapy. Hopefully, she thinks, you will agree, give her permission to drop out of couple work, and take on the challenge of fixing the partner.

And for those who are coasting and marking time, the challenge is greater because the client is saying all the right things, and you usually don't know him well enough to know whether he is sincere in his efforts or not. What you can do is check in regularly about how the therapy is going and listen for signs of ambivalence or challenge any signs of resistance—not doing the homework, showing up late for sessions—ask the hard questions—"I'm wondering if you have mixed feelings about doing this"—and see what emerges.

These can be difficult situations to manage. With the husband who was gay, I had no warning of what was to ensue. For the partner who makes the case for individual therapy, you ultimately have to make your own clinical assessment of what individual therapy the other partner may need, if any (more about that below). In the session, you don't want to take sides, and the best you can often do within the session is to check in with the partner and see if she agrees that individual therapy would be helpful. That said, the partners are still there in the session together; you want to explore what it is they may and can want to accomplish as a couple.

Playing Courtroom. If the drop-off is about one partner cutting and running, leaving you to mop up the emotions, playing courtroom is about placing you on the hot seat. It's exactly what it sounds like. Each partner is presenting evidence—stacking up facts—to make his or her case. What the partners are expecting by the end of the session is a pronouncement by you that one of them is crazy and the other is not, that one is justified in doing what he did (having the affair, calling the police), or whether they should get divorced.

You'll know when this dynamic is unfolding because you will feel assaulted by the endless examples of each other's misbehavior, sometimes going back to childhood and spiked with the hearsay testimony of offsite corroborating witnesses ("My mother just said to me yesterday that you were . . ."). The atmosphere will heat up as each ratchets up the tension, piling on evermore "facts."

It's best to cut off the entire process as soon as you can tell what's happening. As one partner begins to make her case, you can shift the conversation by asking questions about emotions instead of facts, asking questions that evoke a broader perspective ("How have you managed this problem over the years? What's your own theory about what needs to change?"), or you can say flat-out that you feel that they are asking you to be a judge and say who is right and who is wrong. You don't want to do that, you say, because you see your role as helping them to listen to each other better and to untangle the problems between them.

Depending on the emotional climate in the room, you may have to work hard, continually steering them away from facts, actively shaping the conversation. If you can't rein them in and you are feeling overwhelmed by the emotion or content, don't be afraid to separate them.

The expectations that come with the drop-off and playing courtroom shape the first-session process. But there are also a few precipitating events that bring couples into therapy and shape their expectations about what therapy may or may not accomplish. Again, the common ones:

The Big Fight. Fredrico and Paula argue often with lots of screaming and name-calling, but Saturday night was different. Fredrico pushed Paula, causing her to fall over the coffee table and hurt her back. The incident scared both of them and propelled them into seeing you as quickly as possible.

In the initial session, this incident is what they seem to want to talk about most. Fredrico apologizes again and doesn't even blame Paula for his getting so angry. Paula, though teary at times, says she believes that Fredrico is basically a good man, but states clearly that she will not tolerate such physical behavior. Good candidates, you think, for couple therapy: They are motivated and you can help them resolve the underlying issues and teach them the skills they need to avoid such heated arguments in the future.

Good candidates, maybe. Yes, the big fight may scare them both straight enough to fully engage them in therapy, and they may even echo that intention by the end of the session. But what propelled them was the shell-shock of the incident, and for many couples, as that initial fear cools and they have a few weeks of quiet, they drop out. Has much changed? Not likely. But they have gone back to their baseline, their own zone, if not of comfort, then at least of tolerance. They are back to their reality and their own expectations about relationships.

What you can do in the initial session is praise them for taking the risk of coming in, help them each feel safe and heard, and talk about the opportunity that they have to resolve the problems that have been bothering them for so long. In essence, the best you can do is to make it as easy as possible for them to continue and challenge them not to drift back to their baseline.

Affairs. When affairs are uncovered, it is occasionally the wounded partner who comes in alone because the other is refusing to come because she doesn't "do therapy" or feel that it is necessary to repair the relationship, or, as in my case with the husband who was gay, has already left the relationship. But most often both partners will come in. The challenge regarding expectations is exactly that: sorting out expectations not only about therapy, but also about the future of the relationship.

Sometimes, like the best-case scenario for Fredrico and Paula, an affair is a wake-up call for the relationship. The couple realizes the affair was a bad solution to deeper problems in the relationship and both partners are open and clear about what they want to change. It is then merely a matter of clarifying your approach.

But often it is another one-in, one-out situation. The injured partner wants to use therapy to understand what happened, to find a way of building trust again, of seeing what can or what cannot change in the future. The presenting stance of the initiator of the affair is usually one of deep apology, a quick retort that it was all stupid and inexcusable, that it will not happen again, and that he just wants to move forward. What he is hoping for in the session is that you will agree that the apology is sincere, and that yes, it's time to move forward and put it all behind them. The point of therapy, in his mind, is to help the partner get over the emotional upset so life can get back to normal.

Your challenge in the first session is to expand the conversation beyond this "You did–I'm sorry" dialogue. Here is where you can use education to show how affairs are bad solutions to other problems—either within the relationship, the offending individual, or both. You talk about trust being regained and grief (the loss of the sense of the relationship as well as loss of the partner's view of the offender as a person) being resolved *not* by the quick "I'm sorry, let's move on" approach, but by deconstructing the whys for the affair at all. You talk about childhood emotional wounds that have interfered with their being able to express their concerns, be honest, and solve problems for so long.

Here you want not only to support the injured partner, but also to actively work to balance the relationship and conversation by encouraging the offending partner to talk about underlying problems—perhaps the lack of sex, or feeling unappreciated, or the midlife crisis that is screaming that everyday life and visions of the future need to change. Your goal in the initial session is, like courtroom-playing couples, to stay out of the weeds of their content. By the end of the session you want the injured partner to feel that yes, this was emotionally devastating and that her sense of trust is shattered; the offending partner, that mea culpa is appropriate and respected; but that they both have an opportunity to change not only the relationship but their overall approach to problems in their lives.

Addictions. Couples who come to therapy to deal with addictions generally present in one of two ways. In some cases, such as with a pornography or shopping addiction, the behaviors of the offending partner are suddenly discovered—the partner gets busted because the supervisor at work pulled his computer and found the log-ins on porn sites; the credit card bill gets left on the counter inadvertently, revealing the huge charges to different stores. These situations mimic affairs. The injured partner is shell-shocked, grief and trust are the issues in the room, and your goal is that of expanding the conversation beyond the mea culpa over the offense.

Other times there is no sudden disclosure, but rather a partner who is fed up and essentially drags the offending partner to your office. He's worried about how much she has been drinking of late; she's tired of his being stoned all weekend long. Or there is a precipitating event: She drove drunk with the kids in the car; he embarrassed himself in front of her family because he was so high.

The fed-up partner is hoping that you will get the addicted person to see the problem, convince him or her to "grow up" or "see reality," and go into treatment. The addicted partner may respond with denial about the addiction ("Everybody drinks and I go to work everyday"), may minimize the behavior ("I was only driving the kids down the block"), blame the partner for his behavior ("If only you didn't nag so much, I wouldn't have a reason to smoke") or, yes, accept the need for help. Your challenge is to avoid ganging up on the addicted person, but instead to help the injured partner express soft emotions of worry and sadness, rather than anger and frustration. You want to help the addicted person feel safe enough to really hear what the other has to say and to deepen the conversation beyond the "Yes you are–No I'm not" retorts so that each can express more of his or her inner world. Your priority is to change the emotional climate and help the couple decide on possible next steps.

Couple versus Individual

This brings us to the questions of deciding in the first session when, whom, and how to refer out one partner or both for individual therapy, and how to integrate couple therapy into such individual treatments. Depending on your orientation, these issues are only a variation of individual therapy where, as part of your assessment, you decide if and when you might invite others to enter into individual treatment. Here, with couples, you are starting at the other end of the equation and deciding whom to refer out.

Here are some guidelines:

When in Doubt, Refer Out

Always trust your own clinical judgment and instincts. If you suspect that there are individual issues that need to be addressed and could undermine couple treatment, or if you simply suspect something is lurking but don't have time or skill to ferret it out, don't hesitate to refer out—for a medication consult, for example, or for a formal evaluation. Some common concerns:

Addictions. If Nichole is drinking four bottles of wine a night, you don't need to be a clinical genius to see that an addiction problem is at play. And although Nichole may deny she drinks that much or blame her drinking on her partner, the clinical bottom line is that the addiction needs to be addressed and under control before couple work can be successful. So rather than mediating over whose reality is right,

ask Nichole if she is willing to get a substance abuse evaluation just to put the issue to rest. And if Nichole is willing to
begin treatment, hold off on couple work so she can focus on
recovery and get some stability underneath her. Coordinate
with the substance abuse program about when they feel she
might be ready to start couple work again.

Anger. Like addictions, those who struggle with explosive
or violent anger often tend to blame others for causing their
anger. The problem with this stance is that the individual
avoids taking responsibility for his behavior. Referring the client out for help with anger management tools or often underlying post-traumatic stress or anxiety and hypervigilance lets
the client know that you are not going to collude with him in
minimizing the problem but instead take the stand that the
anger needs to be addressed.

If both partners struggle with anger issues, you may decide
to refer both out, or see them separately until they are able to
be together in a session without triggering each other. The
goal of the separate sessions is to identify triggers and teach
self-regulation techniques.

Attention-Deficit/Hyperactivity Disorder. Undiagnosed
or untreated ADHD (attention-deficit/hyperactivity disorder)
can cause havoc in a relationship. Although the partner with
ADHD is struggling to do her best, the other partner is often
at the end of his rope with frustration—bills that don't get
paid, projects that are never finished, appointments forgot-
ten, the clutter, the disorganization. If you suspect ADHD
is at play, refer out for an evaluation. Having a clear diagnosis
can give the couple a new perspective. Rather than the partner being seen as irresponsible or unreliable, she is viewed
through a new lens. Because the effects of medication are gen-

erally rapid, the treatment can quickly change the emotional climate of the relationship.

Individual Mental Health Issues. Individual mental health issues may include severe general anxiety symptoms, OCD, bipolar diagnoses, incapacitating depression, and so on, which require individual treatment and usually medication. Again, coordinate with the individual provider about the client's readiness for couple therapy and again once couple therapy is started, so that you and the other professional are clear about what each is focusing on. This coordination is important to avoid confusing the clients or making it easy for them to split the practitioners. Trust your own clinical instincts and don't be afraid to make your recommendations.

And if a client refuses to comply? You need to decide whether you want to take the strong stand and say, sorry, but you don't feel couple therapy is appropriate at this time, or whether you want to give them a few sessions to build trust and rapport, and see if they can come around to your point of view. Obviously all this depends on your clinical values, orientation, and style.

Couple Therapy and Individual Treatment of One Partner: Don't Do It

The principle of balance enters yet again. Even if you are an addiction specialist, you can't treat Nichole individually and see her with her husband later in the week without him feeling either that (1) yes, indeed, everyone in the room knows who really has the problem and that he is psychologically off the hook; (2) you now know Nichole better than he, have heard much more of her side of the story, and are going to be biased, or both. It's not a good mix.

Decide who your primary client is going to be: the couple or the individual. If the couple, both partners should be seated on your couch most of the time, and if you feel the need to see one separately, see the other separately as well for balance. If you decide to focus on the individual, do so. This doesn't mean that you can't have partners come in periodically to focus on couple issues, but when you do, make sure the goal of the session is specific and limited: for example, to help Nichole map out, with her husband, concrete ways in which he can support her over the holidays when there is much drinking going on around her.

If, on the other hand, you feel that an individual client would benefit from shifting to full-scale couple work, you have two options. One would be to refer the individual client to another therapist who can start the couple work while you continue, or discontinue to see the client individually. The other route is to stop individual work and move toward the couple. The challenge with this option is that you are starting with an unbalanced system, and you will need to balance the system by seeing your client's partner individually for several sessions until rapport, trust, and perspective are established.

Generally, this is most practical if the individual work has been relatively short term. For example, you see Martha initially for depression, but it becomes rapidly clear to you within the first couple of the sessions that her depression is situational, stemming from struggles in her marriage. At that point you invite her husband in, see him for a few sessions, then shift to couple work. If, however, you have been seeing Martha for months, and especially if you are planning to still do some individual work with Martha, it's best to refer them both out to a separate couple therapist.

Because you face forks in the road such as these throughout treatment, and because it is so easy to get caught up in the drama and stories, *and* because balance is so important, it's easy to see how couple work poses challenges that individual treatment does not. The antidote, once again, is your strong leadership and ability to follow the process.

Couple's First Session: Sera and Ben

Sera calls and leaves a voicemail message saying that she received your name from a friend. She'd like to schedule an appointment for couple therapy and is wondering whether you have openings. She leaves her phone number.

Just as we walked through the sessions of Emily and Tom in Chapter 3, let's take a quick walk through the first session with Sera and Ben to put the concepts described above in motion and to highlight the differences from individual treatment. We'll use a cognitive-behavioral and systems treatment framework; as before, try not to get caught up in the clinical issues, but instead focus on the flow and process of the session.

Initial Contact

You call Sera back and she immediately thanks you for responding so quickly. She says again that she got your name from a friend, is wondering if you have any openings, and you say you do. She sighs with relief and then immediately starts saying that she believes her husband, Ben, has been having an emotional affair with a young intern at his job. He denies it, and they had a huge fight about it 2 days ago—their worst ever—and Ben stomped out of the house and didn't return for several hours. They haven't talked much since, but he said he is willing to come in. You say you are sorry to hear this, it must be difficult for them both, and that you'd be happy to see them.

As mentioned earlier, what you don't want to do at this point is press her for more details about the argument or more background information. Why? Because you would be starting therapy without Ben and unbalancing the system. You deliberately say it must be difficult for them *both* for the same reason—to avoid subtly siding with her. Instead you ask if there is anything Sera has particular questions about and she asks about insurance. You refer her to your website to get a better idea of you, your background, and the directions to your office. You set an appointment for the next day.

Although you have little information, your mind is gathering impressions and already mapping out treatment: the way in which the affair may be a bad solution to other problems, questions about how well the partners communicate and solve problems on their own, the fact that their "worst argument ever" didn't involve physical violence or extended separation. You also anticipate the challenges of the upcoming session: that Ben, as the accused, is likely to be defensive, afraid of being judged. And if you are a female therapist, you know that you may need to work hard to offset any likely worry he may have that you will take Sera's side and he will be ganged up on by two women. Similarly, if you are a male therapist, you know you need to offset any worry that Sera may have that you may take her husband's side and minimize the significance of his behavior.

Part 1a: The Opening. Both partners appear to be in their mid-30s. They sit together on the couch (a good sign, rather than sitting apart in separate chairs). Ben came from work, is dressed in a jacket and tie; Sera came from the gym in casual clothes. Sera is leaning forward, Ben seems huddled in the couch corner.

You thank them for coming, ask if they had a chance to look at your website. Sera said she did; Ben, in a quiet voice, says he didn't get a chance to do so. You use that as an opportunity to introduce yourself and experience. You ask if they have been in counseling before, and Sera says that they only did premarital counseling through their church before marriage.

"Let me get some quick background," you say. How long married: 7 years. Children: two, ages 6 and 4. Jobs: Sera works part-time from home doing web design. Ben is a manager at a software development company. You ask more about his work—how did he get into the field, what he does day to day—to draw him out and hopefully warm him up. After a few minutes he speaks a bit louder and seems more relaxed. You also note the red flag of their 7-year marriage: possible 7-year itch.

Part 1b: Client Story. "Tell me what brings you here," and, as expected, Sera speaks up. "I've been feeling for a while that we seemed disconnected. Ben works long hours, I'm tied up with all the kids' stuff—the after-school activities and the house as well as my job. But the other night I noticed Ben's phone on the coffee table—he had just gotten that phone last week—and I picked it up just to look at it and see what was different about it, and it opened up to text messages. There I saw a long trail of messages between him and Ashley from work, and they clearly weren't just about work—he was talking about how he too felt trapped at times and that it's hard to talk to me. . . ." She starts to tear up.

Ben jumps in: "Look," he says, "I wasn't trying to hurt you, but you are making a big deal about nothing." He puts his hand on her shoulder; his voice sounds more frustrated than angry. "Ashley was talking about trouble she was having with her boyfriend. She sees me as some mentor, and I was just trying to be sympathetic, saying I felt the same way at times."

"But, this was intimate," snaps back Sera. "You were talking to her about things you have never talked to me about—that's why I'm hurt." She tears up again and grabs a tissue.

So where are you so far? You're 10 minutes into the session. In terms of time, you're fine. You note that Sera is a kinesthetic person—*feel, sense*—while Ben is a visualizer—*see, look.* You want to be empathic toward Sera but also not ask questions that take her further down the road of her tears, which could dominate the emotional climate and the time. Ben has spoken up, so we don't need to work any more to draw him out. He has acknowledged her hurt, which means he is not totally on the defensive, and they're not swinging into playing courtroom and squabbling over whose reality is right. Clinically, Sera's comment is on target—why couldn't he tell her how he felt? Does he feel the same disconnection that she mentioned at the start? If this opening up to Ashley is a bad solution, what is the problem in the relationship or with each of them as individuals?

"So," you ask Sera gently, "you just said that it was the intimacy of the conversation that hurt you most. Can you say more about that?" You don't want to stir up her emotions as much as help her clearly express to Ben why or what is most upsetting for her before moving on to him.

"I guess, as I said before, we've been disconnected. I focus on the kids, Ben with work; we seem to be in two separate worlds. We don't have or make time for us, and we don't talk much, but now he's opening up and talking to someone else." (No further tears; good).

"So Ben," you say quietly, "have you heard this before? Do you see what Sera is saying?"

"Yeah, I do. Again, I want to say that this wasn't an emotional affair." *(Sera doesn't counter; good; he sounds less frustrated).* "Ashley is a young intern who looks up to me. Our relationship has been strictly professional, but in our last supervisory meeting, when I asked why she seemed more withdrawn lately, she mentioned problems with the boyfriend. I just listened. And yes, we do text about work stuff. So she mentioned the boyfriend thing again the next day in the text, and, like I said, I was trying to be supportive. That's it. It's not some big ongoing relationship. Yeah, maybe I shouldn't have shared so much, but there was nothing behind it."

"I guess I'm wondering," you say, "if you felt the way Sera has—disconnected as a couple?"

"Sure, I'm busy, she's busy. Welcome to the 21st century." Hmm, now he sounds depressed.

"You sound kind of down as you say that. How are you feeling right now?"

"I don't know . . . I thought that at this point in our lives, we'd be in a different place, less preoccupied maybe, closer."

Okay, you're out of the woods. No long rant about Sera from Ben, no escalating argument, no stacking of evidence. The emotional climate has shifted from potential anger and accusation to a sad calm. The process seems balanced—Ben has been able as much as Sera to be open—the rapport and safety are there. More importantly, they are emotionally in the same place and there is a common problem: disconnection from each other.

Part 2: Assessment. It is time for you to shift focus and, depending on your clinical orientation, ask whatever you need to ask to connect the dots and develop and confirm your hypothesis. You ask about how each of them has changed over the 7 years they have been married. You ask about good times, positive memories to help change the emotional climate, about their parents and their marriages. You're tracking whether the conversation becomes more open as they each speak. You're looking for matches and mismatches between the nonverbal and verbal cues—the hesitant yes, the sigh or glare or a pulling away—and you address them as they come up: "You just sighed Ben, why?"; "I noticed your physically pulling back, Sera—what just happened?" You're trying to help them fill out the conversation by giving words to these nonverbal signals; you're asking questions to make the conversation deeper and more intimate.

And you stay alert for possible transference clues as you move through the process. Sera mentions a critical father from whom she withdrew; Ben is able to clearly say that he feels that Sera is always questioning, suspicious of his actions, and not unlike his mom, not very affectionate. You mentally map out for yourself what not to do to trigger these reactions: avoid sounding critical toward Sera; avoid coming off as interrogative, micromanaging or detached to Ben.

But you still haven't nailed down the larger clinical issues: namely, what keeps them from working out these problems on their own? Why is Ben telling a colleague what he can't say to his own wife? What keeps Ben and Sera, who both admit to feeling disconnected from each other, from voicing their unhappiness and finding a way together of changing it?

"Ben," you say, "one of the things you said in the text to Ashley that hurt Sera's feelings was about Sera not knowing that you felt trapped. What do you mean by that?"

"Just that I'm not only feeling burned out at work but that

I also feel like I'm stuck. Financially we're hemmed in. I can't imagine being able to do anything different with my job until the kids get older and Sera can go back to work full-time."

"But it looks like this has been bothering you for a while. What's the other part: How come you haven't talked about this?"

"Well, part of the problem is that we never seem to have a good time. Like I said, she's busy, I'm busy, she's tired, I'm tired. We do a lot with the kids when we're together, like on the weekends."

"But you're both saying that you feel disconnected. I'm wondering why you don't bring it up to let her know how you feel."

"I guess sometimes I feel that Sera's not interested. She never asks me about me."

Sera flares: "I never ask because you're always in your own head! Do you ever really ask anything about me!"

Ben shrugs and looks down. You're watching the clock; you have 10 minutes left. If you had more time you could coax Ben to respond, help them use the safety of the session to start the conversation that they need to have at home but don't. But right now, you need to bring this together and present the treatment plan. Both partners have done a good job of getting the issues on the table in a balanced way.

Part 3a: Present the Treatment Plan. "I'm looking at the time," you say, "and realize that we only have few minutes left. I appreciate your both coming today. We started out talking about the text message to Ashley. Ben, do you understand why Sera's so upset about it?"

"Yeah, I do. Like I said, there wasn't anything more than that. I don't want Sera to feel that there is some relationship starting or going on."

"Yeah, I believe you," says Sera, now calmer. "I'm just worried about us."

This is good; through the process of the session, they've been able to move the emotional affair issue to the back burner. You can move forward.

"In my way of thinking, I tend to consider most problems as bad solutions to some other underlying problem. Affairs of any kind are usually just that: a bad solution to a relationship problem, an individual problem, or both. That's not to condone the behavior or minimize the hurt that it can cause, but to help put the problem in a different context so the real issues can be addressed. You've both talked today about feeling disconnected from each other, not having time as a couple, each of you essentially living parallel lives—Ben, in your work, Sera, with the children. If it's difficult to talk to each other for whatever reason, problems don't get solved, distance becomes a way of avoiding conflict, and both partners can feel resentful and lonely. But rather than breaking the code of silence, it's easier to simply pull away more, making the problems worse."

You look to see if they are with you, and they both are nodding their heads. What you are doing here is normalizing their experience, using education to connect their initial concerns with the larger landscape, and thereby further changing the climate in the room.

"You've also been married 7 years, and you both have said how different you are from when you first married. There really is a 7-year itch where couples can feel that the relationship has changed and isn't working." You then go on to briefly explain the 7-year-itch process, using education here as well to normalize their experience. Again, they seem to be tracking with you.

"So your challenge is to move your relationship from the

back burner to the front . . . to make time for each other, but also take the risk of talking about things that you have avoided talking about—affection, verbal intimacy, finances, your visions of the future. That's what we can work on here. Does all this make sense?"

"It does to me," says Sera. "I can see how my being so preoccupied with the kids has created this gap between us."

"Ben, what you are thinking?"

"I'm thinking that it is hard for me to talk to Sera probably because of *me*. She's right, I do tend to just keep things in my head."

"It's good you're aware of that. I believe that recognizing a problem is halfway toward solving it. We just need to help you change those habits."

"That would be good."

Part 3b: Homework and Next Steps. There is consensus and balance all around and no objections to counter. Time to give them homework. You ask them to both think of three things they would like the other person to do differently in a very concrete and specific way—not, for example, *listen better,* but actually figure out what listening better would look like so the other person knows exactly what to do differently. They both say they can do that. You set the next appointment.

This session flowed well because both partners showed self-awareness, a willingness to self-disclose, and were able to regulate their emotions and avoid getting lost in content. But you were able to do the same—keep Sera from getting teary and dominating the session with her hurt, helping Ben feel safe enough and not ganged up upon to speak up.

If it were otherwise—escalation, denial, and blame—you

would have had to step up, control the process, have them do monologues to control interruptions, press for softer emotions, or possibly separate them. You might have run into trouble with managing the time, you might have had to follow up with one of the partners if you felt the session was left unbalanced. But thanks to your leadership, and luck perhaps, both partners feel better when they leave than when they came in; both have a new perspective on the issues; both are willing to return. A good session, all around.

CHAPTER 6

First Sessions with Families

Chris is the father of an 8-year-old son, Joel, who has been having trouble in school. His teachers are complaining that Joel is "fidgety," interrupts, and doesn't complete his work in class, and Chris admits to having problems with Joel at home. He and his wife Kim would like to come in with Joel, and even his older brother, Nat, if you think that would be helpful.

Abby calls. She's worried about her 16-year-old daughter Chloe. Chloe has this "negative attitude" all the time, blows up over nothing, her grades are sliding, and her current boyfriend is a 16-year-old who is constantly in trouble at school and thinking of dropping out. Abby is at her wit's end.

FAMILY THERAPY: WE think of children in various sizes and ages, teens who are acting out or depressed, parents like Abby feeling fed up and overwhelmed. But families can also be grown children with elderly parents, 20-something siblings who don't get along, new parents who lack the skills or confidence to manage their new baby or a rambunctious toddler.

In this chapter we are going to discuss the ins and outs of

first sessions with families, using those of Chris and Abby to map the family therapy terrain.

The Landscape of Family Therapy

Just as we oriented ourselves to couple work by looking at its broad landscape, let's do the same for family therapy:

More People, More Problems

Family therapy is often terrifying for beginning therapists because they automatically imagine six people in a room, including the family dog, all vying for attention, all presenting a different slant on a handful of different problems. Although this can certainly happen, it need not be as terrifying as it seems.

One reason is that family therapy is actually easier than couple therapy because the dreaded triangle in the room is eliminated. Although balance is still important in family therapy—you don't want to leave someone out or have anyone feel ganged up on—families create their own momentum, which makes the running of the process easier. Your role here is more like that of a traffic cop—signaling Dad to move forward to describe his view of the problem, holding up your hand to the sister signaling the right of way to someone else, then stopping the dad so that the mom and teenager can both come ahead and have their say.

But the other reason family therapy need not be so arduous as imagined is that family therapy is not about cramming as many folks as possible into a room, but more a way of thinking about problems—systemic, psychodynamic—whatever your perspective. If the six (or three or four) seem too overwhelming, you can always break the family down into smaller chunks. Here are some of the common format options to consider:

Total Family Session. This is where you do bring in the live-in grandma and the daughter home from college, and anybody else that makes up the family. The advantage here is that you can get multiple perspectives and are able to see the entire family in action—the organic machine with no parts missing. The downside is that you have multiple perspectives and can see the entire family in action, and this is where those feelings of being overwhelmed take hold. But if you take charge, act the traffic cop, and are clear about your own agenda and goals, this kind of session can turn out well and save you time down the road to boot.

Working with the Parents Alone. Here you tell Chris to get a babysitter for Joel and come in with Kim, or ask Abby to come in by herself for the first session before inviting Chloe. Though you have to be mindful of staying balanced with Chris and Kim as a couple, you have fewer people to focus on, and this format makes it easier for you to gather specific information you feel you need. This may involve covering Joel's developmental history, for example, without his being in the room, or exploring the parents' childhoods.

But most helpful about this format is that you have the time and space to drill down and determine where the parents may be getting stuck in solving their parenting problem on their own. Is it the result of learning problems—lack of skill or information—or problems about learning—their own emotions interfering with ability to utilize their skills? Is it because the parents are not on the same page and working together as a team? There are some schools of thought that most family problems are, at their heart, marital problems.

Even if that is not completely or always the case, parents who are at odds around parenting are, at best, sending confusing messages to the children, canceling each other out, and weakening the family structure.

Working with the Identified Patient and the Parents. Chris, Kim, and Joel come in and the brother stays home; Abby and Chloe show up for the first session. As when working with parents alone, this combination allows you the time— you don't need to build rapport with Joel's brother—to focus on the presenting problem. The downside is that you may miss what Nat has to offer—his worry about the parents' marriage, for example; or how he too struggles with the same problems as Joel, though he copes differently; or that he knows that Joel is being bullied at school without teachers and parents realizing it.

Working with the Identified Patient Alone. At the beginning stages of the family therapy movement, many institutes adopted the child-study model whereby children and parents were seen separately—often a psychologist or child specialist seeing only the child, a social worker seeing the parents. For those clinicians who are particularly skilled with children or simply prefer to do individual child work, this treatment team approach is often preferred, and this format is still used in many psychiatric hospitals. The clear focus is obvious. The downside is not seeing the interactions between parent and child, as well as the challenge of tightly coordinating the separate work of the clinicians.

A practical middle ground is seeing the identified patient (IP) alone for a portion of a first session with parents or the total family. It can give you a brief opportunity to gather your own first impressions of the child, build rapport through play therapy with younger children, or show a teen that you are not another authoritarian adult and are interested in understanding the teen's individual goals.

Working with Sibling Groups. It would be unusual for a first session to include only a group of siblings, but occasionally it happens—siblings, for example, who are newly placed together in foster care. But it is conceivable that you might break off the sibling group just as you might break off the IP as part of first session. The advantage of seeing a sibling group is that you not only see the interaction among the siblings and get a more rounded picture of the family from their perspective, but if there is one child who is younger or shy, the other siblings can provide the support that helps that child feel safe and open up.

The point in looking at these combinations is to realize that there are multiple ways of starting family therapy. What you choose will depend on your clinical orientation, your comfort zone, and often simple logistics: who is available in the family to come in at any given time.

Working with Different Ages

If Joel's brother Nat is 12, you'll be talking to him in a different way than you will be talking to Joel; you'll be focusing on different topics to build rapport. Ditto if you have 3-year-old and an 80-year-old grandmother in the same room. This isn't a major clinical challenge, but it does require that you know about, and are comfortable relating to, the different developmental stages of your clients.

Strong Leadership . . . Again

The need for your strong leadership with couples is to maintain the balance and keep their ability to push emotional buttons from dissolving the session into chaos. Although the balance issue is less strong with families, the potential button-pushing behavior and seeming chaos remain. You generally want to let families "run" at their normal pace and process, so that you can observe the patterns and interactions—do the parents step in and keep Joel from interrupting, or do you need to speak up?—but you never want to let go of the reins of the process. If you do, you will soon feel overwhelmed and wind up spending valuable time trying to corral them all. Again, your own self-confidence and a clear roadmap are your best antidotes to these challenges.

Clear Treatment Maps

As with individuals and couples, before the first session you want to have a clear mental roadmap for how you might run the session, as well as anticipate the treatment maps you might use to address the family's problems. The fact that more people mean more problems (at least potentially) indicates that you'll need to brainstorm individual and relational issues that may arise. As you hear Chris's description of Joel's behavior, for example, you may be thinking *ADHD*, but realize it may also reflect an agitated depression or Joel's response to bullying or other trauma. Chloe too may be struggling with depression or oppositional defiant disorder (ODD), but the real problem, you know from experience, may be Abby's struggle to set limits and structure, which then makes you curious about the skill and emotional issues that prevent Abby from doing so. This type of anticipating and brainstorming helps you frame your assessment, as well as mentally hold the treatment maps at the ready.

If you will be working with or assessing small children, part of your treatment map will undoubtedly be some form of play therapy. Here too you want to clinically clarify ahead of time how you might use the play therapy—as an assessment tool, as a primary form of treatment—so you can build that into your pitch to the parents, as well as helping you prepare on a practical level by having the right supplies and space you need to meet a child at a specific age.

Clear Guidelines for Referring Out

If you don't have skills in play therapy—or if Abby says that Chloe has, in fact, been getting pot from her boyfriend, suspects she is smoking throughout the day, and you have no real knowledge of drug addictions—you may suggest a play therapist referral for the young child and an addiction specialist's evaluation for Chloe. If Chris mentions that the school psychologist said, at some early teacher conference, that she was concerned about "autistic tendencies" and this is outside your practice range, you may want to send Chris and Joel to a developmental pediatrician before coming to see you. If Abby mentions that she has a long history of OCD, and that at times (like now) it interferes with her ability to parent Chloe, and this disorder is totally outside your clinical range, you may want to speak with her about finding an individual therapist to help her.

We're back to the issue we discussed with couples: namely, when and how to refer out to, and combine, individual treatment with your family work. Your skill and orientation are clearly determinants, and part of treatment planning will be deciding whether the individual work should take precedence over the family work or whether individual and family work can be done concurrently.

The rule of thumb is that if the individual issues will undermine the family treatment—that Joel may not be able to cognitively process what his parents are asking, or Abby's internal obsessions will distract from her ability to set and maintain structure—an evaluation or the start of individual treatment will take precedence. Similarly, to address Chloe's marijuana smoking, you may recommend that she be evaluated for possible substance abuse addiction, and if found addicted, that she begin treatment before any family therapy takes place. Conversely, if it is determined that Chloe's smoking is largely a reaction to the stress in the family, that Joel is found to *not* be on the autism spectrum but only has ADHD that can likely be managed by tighter behavioral regimen, or that Abby's OCD can be significantly reduced with medication, you now know you can put those doubts and concerns out of your mind and confidently move ahead.

Transference–Countertransference Issues

You'll be looking for the transference clues for each individual family member—don't sound critical of Chris, perhaps, or don't pepper his wife Kim with too many questions that leave her feeling overwhelmed and on the spot; don't sound scolding to Joel—all no different from what you do with individuals and couples. But what makes this easier to determine in family therapy is that, in contrast to individuals where you're forced to look for clues through content and history, these old wounds are often played out in the mix of interactions there in the room. You hear Kim make a relatively innocuous comment to Chris, and he becomes defensive right there and then. Chris peppers Kim with questions about what the teacher said exactly, and she shuts down. Kim snaps at Joel and he turns away and pulls in. The behaviors and patterns unfold before you, offering you the opportunity to step in and once again be the ideal parent.

But there is always the other side of the therapeutic coin—countertransference—and here with families it can be more complicated. Suppose you are 28 years old, single, no children. Chris comes in, and in his authoritarian manner, reminds you of your controlling dad, or Abby looks you up and down and asks at the start whether you have kids. Your own emotional reactions can come into play, and you find yourself being less confrontive with Chris than you might ordinarily be, you find yourself stammering a retort to Abby's question, and you worry throughout the rest of the session if she is going to mentally dismiss anything you might suggest.

This tangle of countertransference reactions can, of course, arise in individual therapy, but what makes family therapy a bit different is that you have a wider range of generations that can trigger these countertransference reactions—your sensitivity to Abby or the danger of your overidentifying with Joel or Chloe. Your antidote, as it is with all countertransference, is self-awareness—realizing that being single with no children is apt to raise eyebrows with some clients and that that doesn't diminish your expertise—and preparedness—anticipating before Chris shows up or Abby asks her questions what your response will be. Here is also where supervision or consultation with a trusted colleague can help by aiding you in uncovering your own reactions, as well as giving you tools with which to counter them in the session.

Heightened Resistance Issues

We talked earlier about situations in which the courts have determined that the parents are abusive, but the parents feel that what they are doing what's necessary, God-given, or within their inherent rights to do; and families in which the parents, because of their strong family values, absolutely do not believe in medication or in teenagers dating before they are 18. When meeting such families you are immediately faced with a clash of cultures—yours and the community versus those of the family. Your challenge is to find a way of integrating your clinical perspective into the culture of the family. So you clarify and correct expectations; you link your assessment and treatment plan to the family's presenting problem and primary concerns; you help the family not confuse the means with the goal—that therapy is merely one way of addressing the court's ultimate concern that the abusive behaviors in the home stop. Most of all you find some common ground on which to move forward—which in some cases may be the family wanting to get the court off their backs.

Similarly, there are those children or teens who, because of anxiety or resentment at being dragged in by parents, refuse to talk or become oppositional in the session. All these scenarios represent the times that family therapy, unlike individuals or even couples, can be more challenging. Your goal, as with resistant adults, is to neutralize their initial resistance with rapport, safety, and being the ideal parent. You create motivation by uncovering a goal on which they are willing to work.

Heightened Motivation as Resource

Yes, the motivation for therapy can vary among the individuals in the family and resistance can spring up, but generally family therapy is not all doom and gloom; in fact, clients who come for family therapy are often more motivated. Although there is still some one-in, one-out aspect to family therapy, wherein one parent is less enthralled with the therapy than the other, generally both parents are motivated to help their kids—because they want the best for them, because they are tired of hearing complaints from the school. Teens genuinely want help in getting their parents to understand what they want, and younger children sincerely are hoping that their father will not yell at them all the time. Those in family therapy often lack the ambivalence that you may find with couples who are confused about their overall feelings regarding the relationship or using therapy to solve problems. And even in other family therapy variations—where grown children are worrying about elderly parents living alone and potentially breaking hips—the motivation for change is strong. This is good. It makes your first session work easier.

Changing the Emotional Climate

Your challenge remains the same: Families should leave your office feeling better than when they came in. As with other aspects of the family process, this too may be easier to create in this format than with individuals or couples. A young child may feel fine by the end of the session simply because you seemed "nice"; a teen feels better simply because you didn't act like her father and rant at her for the entire session; parents are relieved to leave with new information to help them see their problem in a new way.

Because there are family triggers and shifts that you cannot yet be aware of, the actual changing of the climate is often more subtle in family work. Joel, with your coaxing, actually gets to say how he feels at school, finally feels listened to and understood; and his parents, to whom he rarely opens up, hear another side of him and are touched. Similarly, Abby, as a single parent who feels so alone in her struggles as a parent, through your active listening (and in spite of your age), leaves with a sense that someone finally understands her worry. Or Chloe, without massive effort on your part, doesn't see you as yet another adult telling her she needs to ditch her boyfriend because you deliberately don't. Although she still may be wary, she is more relaxed and feels safe; the fearful expectations she was bracing herself for have not materialized and with a big sigh of relief on her part, she discovers that you are not like her mother.

This is the momentum of family therapy that makes this type of therapeutic work easier. You step up to be the ideal parent and partner all around. Listen to Abby and don't criticize (which she is expecting and fears), help Joel feel listened to, empathize with Chris and Kim about their concern as parents for Joel. And if the more dramatic happens—Kim begins to cry, Chloe gets overwhelmed and walks out—be ready, map out this possibility ahead of time—how to mop up, how to link whatever happens to the clients' concerns.

Here too education becomes a strong tool for emotional change. As mentioned earlier, think of the family doctor who quells your fears by explaining that what you've imagined (and what WebMD has suggested) is not true. Chris and Kim, who are struggling to understand why Joel has such a hard time at home and school and likely blame themselves in some way, who may worry about the autism word being spoken, take comfort when you explain that in your opinion Joel may have ADHD, which causes him to be impulsive and hyperactive. Similarly, Abby feels relieved when she hears you explain that some of Chloe's oppositional behavior is not uncommon for teens her age, that it is part of individuation, and not the end result of her parenting.

The changes we find, then, in the overall clinical landscape of families are those of a higher level of complexity. Just as couple work introduces the dynamics of the two-person interaction and need for balance, families present the multilayered problems, the tracking and guiding of process with more individuals in the room, the wider array of possible presenting problems, the more complex issues of transference and countertransference. But the core elements remain the same: of leadership, of tracking the process, of being prepared, of changing the emotional climate.

We're about ready to move on to the first-session family process, but before we do, we need talk more specifically about that other major difference between families and couples or individuals: namely, the world of children and teens and their impact on the clinical dynamics. We'll take these topics one by one.

Children in Therapy

Every family is unique, of course, but here are some of the challenges that children can pose in the first session:

More Chaos

Even if you are not doing total family therapy with a range of ages in the room, children are not adults, nor are older teens. They can get restless and fidget or become bored. They can feel left out or intimidated or can be jockeying among themselves for your or the parent's attention. Because their verbal and self-regulation skills are less strong, they can act out their problems—becoming angry or agitated or tearful much more easily. And if the parents need to bring a baby, you'll have to prepare yourself not only for a range of eruptions that the baby may create, but for the baby's strong distractive pull, interfering with the flow of the session.

Decide on your own comfort and policy regarding the inclusion of babies or toddlers in the session. Sometimes you can arrange appointments for the baby's naptime, or a non-IP sibling can take the baby out to the waiting room if the baby becomes upset. Parents can often bring toys and blankets to place on the floor, extra bottles, etc. Discuss options and scenarios and your own limits before the session so parents have clear expectations.

Young children may need to have something to engage with while they listen to the family conversation. If space permits, you may want to create some play space in the room, such as a small child-sized table in the corner of the room where they can color, draw, or play with plastic animals; if not, have some materials available even if the children play on the floor. Again, if feeling unsure, talk with the parents ahead of time so they can brainstorm with you ways to minimize distractions. Also map out in advance Plans A and B through a mix of formats: Start out in total family therapy, for example, then shift to seeing the parents alone and sending the kids out to the waiting room to play games on their iPads; or shift to play therapy for the second half of the session if a child becomes too restless.

If possible issues of misbehavior arise—a child yelling or getting aggressive, constantly interrupting, mistreating your toys, threatening to leave the room—it's best to see what the parents do or don't do first to deal with the child. This gives you clues to their parenting style, tolerance for misbehavior, and ability to set limits. But you're the leader, so if the parents seem unable to set appropriate limits, don't be afraid to ask them to take action: Take their child out of the room, place the child in a time-out by sitting on a chair in the corner, or take away the toy that the child is misusing.

Two-Tiered Conversations

Although you need to build rapport with each child in the room and ask direct questions at their verbal level to gather the information you need, you can often talk over the heads of young children (ages 2–6 years) to have somewhat separate conversations with parents. You can ask about "coping skills" or "overall relationship with teachers" or "their marital stressors," for example, and even let parents know that this level of conversation is exactly what you want to do at that moment. When it's time to bring the children into the conversation, you can simplify your vocabulary and talk directly to the child. An example:

"So I understand that your daughter had some testing done through the school. What were the results?"

"Well, they were concerned about some possible learning disabilities and found that she may have a learning disability that affects her ability to process math concepts."

"Cassie, you're mom just said that you sometimes have a hard time with math. Is math hard for you?"

Words such as *daughter, testing, results,* and *concepts* are likely to go by Cassie. You deliberately do not say her name—"I understand that Cassie had testing"—since this will likely trigger Cassie and create anxiety. Again, track the process and watch Cassie. If she shows signs of concern, reduce her anxiety by helping her understand, at her verbal level, what the conversation is about.

Children Feel Safe if the Parents Feel Safe

Young children, although more verbally limited, are also more sensitive to feeling tone in the room, especially those cues generated by their parents. If the parents seem relaxed and safe in your presence, the child will likely come to feel the same. What this point translates to in practical terms is the importance of not only setting the tone and creating safety with the parents, but of spending some time with parents and child together before deciding to see the child briefly alone in play therapy or conversation.

Tweens

Because children vary in their development, you will find some 11-year-olds who still engage best through some modified play therapy, whereas there are 9-year olds who are fine having a session-long conversation. Part of your assessment during the first session is judging the developmental age of the "tween" child. Is he able to sit still and engage in conversation, or is he easily bored or distracted or having a difficult time tracking the discussion? You can generally gather this information through observation within the first 10 minutes of the session.

Parents as Therapists

Although this is a question of clinical orientation, many pre-teens with behavioral problems can be effectively treated by their parents. If you consider, for example, what treatment children are usually given in residential programs, it is the firm structure with clear consequences and rewards that help them learn to self-regulate and change behaviors. For behavioral issues that are not extreme, and especially when children are very young (ages 2–6 years), helping parents to do the same is often all that is needed.

If you decide to take this route, you'll hold the first session with the parents alone. You'll focus on defining the troublesome behaviors, the possible triggers, what the parents have done that has worked and not worked in the past, and then coaching parents on how to concretely approach these problems in the home. Here you may need to tell parents specifically what to say to their child and how to behaviorally and emotionally respond to triggers and the child's actual behavior, making sure that both parents are onboard and leave knowing exactly what to do. Follow-up sessions would focus on what worked and did not work over the course of the week and fine-tuning the treatment plan. If several weeks of this approach net little or no improvement, you can then shift to Plan B, whereby either you or another therapist sees the child for assessment and possible play therapy to deal with underlying emotional issues.

As an example of this approach, suppose Scott and Kirsten come in concerned about their 5-year-old son's anxiety at bedtime. For the last several weeks, he seems particularly sensitive to noises, shadows, and possible monsters. The parents put him in bed following his bedtime routine of snack, bath, and books, but within minutes of their leaving the room, he cries out that he is scared. The parents come in, reassure him, show him that there are no monsters, and so forth. He seems to calm down but again minutes later, he is crying out again. Now 2 weeks later they are worn out and finding that the only way to get him to sleep is to have one of them sleep alongside him in his bed for several hours.

In the first session with the parents you explore possible reasons for this current anxiety—changes at home or school—

and, finding no outstanding triggers, coach the parents on how to respond. What has happened, you realize, is that their son has trained them to be his remedy for his anxiety—they leave, he gets anxious, cries out, they come in or sleep with him and he calms down; their child is controlling the process. What they need to do instead is acknowledge his anxiety (rather than minimize or dismiss it), but take charge of the process. What this means is that they settle him in bed, say that they are going to check on him in 5 minutes, and actually check on him in 3.

The idea is to reassure him before his anxiety ramps up. The child's anxiety is reduced by their proactively checking in before it reaches such high levels, and the child learns that the parents are indeed on duty and available, helping him to feel safe and relax. Gradually over the course of a few nights they increase the time between check-ins, and they give him lots of praise the next morning for doing so well. Generally within a few days of this practice, their son's anxiety is likely to have lessened, and you bypass the need to see the child, develop rapport, and drag out the length of treatment.

Adolescents in Therapy

Whereas the child's dependence on parents shapes the process of working with them in and out of the family session, adolescents' counterdependence—their bouncing away from parents as part of individuation—creates a different landscape. Again, the common factors:

Teens Are More Articulate

Unless they are intellectually challenged, teens, unlike young children, are able to have longer conversations and grasp concepts and principles. That said, given that adolescents' pre-frontal lobes are not fully developed, their rational thinking and ability to process emotions are still limited. This is why parents' extended lectures about the future often fall on deaf ears, or why many teens become easily overwhelmed and have a difficult time seeing their situation from a larger perspective.

What this developmental stage means in clinical terms is that, whereas you need to simplify your questions or set up yes-and-no responses from children, with teens you can ask more detailed questions, track the problem under the prob-lem, and encourage them to describe the specific thoughts and emotions beneath their actions. Although their age pre-vents you from talking over their heads, it does enable you to deepen the conversation in the room. Not only does this help the parents gain a more rounded picture of what the teen is actually thinking and feeling, the new level of conversation itself can change the emotional climate.

Teens Can Be More Resistant

Children who seem resistant to coming are generally anx-ious—about meeting a stranger in a strange place, worrying that they are in trouble, or because they are unsure of what to expect. Although teens can certainly feel this way as well, what fuels their resistance more is their counterdependence stance: being sensitive to authority and being told what to do. Many teens feel railroaded into coming, like Chloe, who, although her mother seems to be having a problem with her behavior, feels she is doing fine and only wants to be left alone. So she comes reluctantly and is silent or visibly angry.

Your simply being an adult doesn't help this, and being an adult with authority who is ostensibly trying to get them to change helps even less. What you most want to avoid in the first session is being perceived as joining with the parent and ganging up on the teen. There are several ways to avoid doing this.

One is to be honest and say aloud to the teen what you believe you and he are both thinking: that you're worried that he's afraid that you'll join the parent in ganging up on him, that you will judge his mental health, or that you'll push him to do what he doesn't want to do. You say that you are there not to take sides but to help them, as a family, solve the problems between them, and that you really want to know from his perspective just what those problems are. You want to be sensitive to how you sound and even your posture—do not seem to loom over the teen—especially if sitting close by. Finally, if you feel that any of these approaches is not working, ask the parent to leave and spend some time, one on one, building rapport and changing the emotional climate by having a more intimate conversation.

Greater Potential for Emotional Drama with Teens

Although younger children may misbehave in a session, this can usually be handled through some behavioral management: the parents giving warnings or setting limits, or you redirecting the child toward some activity such as drawing. With the teen's greater verbal ability comes the potential for heated exchanges, not unlike that of couples. Your task, as mentioned in the last chapter, is to manage the process. Have one person talk at a time, ask one to talk to you rather than the other person, focus on soft emotions rather than anger. And if the process escalates too quickly and intensely, separate the parents and the teen so you are not replicating the patterns into which they so easily fall.

A common scenario with teens and parents that often

unfolds is that the parents attack as soon as you ask the family members why they are here: "We're here because of her attitude"; We're here because of what happened Saturday night"; and all their frustration spews forth, backed by heaps of evidence and incidences to back up their claims and emotions. The critical factor here for you is what happens next: namely, is the teen able to defend herself and counterattack or does she simply shut down?

The teen who is able to push back against this verbal assault is showing strength and resiliency, making for a fairly even playing field. Your task then is that of managing the process, curtailing escalation, helping the family change the conversation by focusing on softer emotions, and if necessary, separating parents and teen to stop the escalation. But if instead the teen is overwhelmed, shuts down, and is getting emotionally clobbered by the parents, everything is unbalanced and you need to step in and stop it. If you don't, you are not only replicating the problem in the room, but you are, by your inaction, sanctioning the parents' assault. Rather than feeling safe, the teen feels unsafe; rather than seeing you as a not-parent, you are, in fact, seen as one of them. Any possibility of rapport is shattered, and the teen has no reason to trust you or come back.

So as with violent couples, you call a halt. You ask the teen if it would be okay to talk with her by herself. The teen will usually shrug an okay. You ask the parents if they wouldn't mind going to the waiting room and say that you will talk with them in a few minutes. They leave, thinking that you will do your magic and say something that will straighten the teen out. You then slouch in your seat and say in a gentle voice, "Wow, is this what they always do? Are you okay?"

What you've done in the teen's eyes is acknowledge the

emotional beating she's just received and have stopped the attack. Your goal at this point is simple: To get the teen to talk. Again, you are the not-parent, and you don't want the teen to shut down as she just did with the parents, but instead to open up. The content isn't important. Your goal is to change the emotional climate. Ask about parents, but also ask about school or friends or dating or sports or hobbies; listen to the intricacies of her latest videogame if necessary; the point is to create conversation. Yes, you can raise the parents' concerns but restate them in softer terms: "It seems like your parents are really worried about what happened Saturday night. Did it bother you? How do you think about it differently?"

What you're trying to do here is build a separate and different adult relationship, creating the experience of a different conversation with an adult, one where she feels safe. You are looking for a problem, and hence the motivator, that the teen defines that will give the teen a reason to continue with therapy: "I want my parents get off my back"; "I want to spend more time with my dad"; "I want my parents to stop arguing." Usually the parents' and teen's problems are interconnected; if the parents back off or Dad spends more time with the teen or the parents argue less, the teen's attitude will improve. You can now redefine expectations: The family therapy will need to address the parents' concerns, but will also be a safe forum in which to focus on the teen's agenda. Track the process to see if the teen is onboard. If not, back up and repair.

But don't forget the clock. The parents have been sitting in the waiting room for 10 minutes. You need some closure with them. Ask the teen if it's okay if you see the parents by themselves. You assure her that you will not discuss what she just talked about—this is between you and her, but you want to touch base with them to see if they have any questions. The teen will shrug okay, and you send her out.

What do you say to the parents? You say you are sorry you needed to send them out, but you were worried that their teen was getting overwhelmed and the one-on-one time allowed you to connect. The parents are relieved because their biggest worry was that their daughter wouldn't like you and would refuse to come back. Depending on time, you then tell them what will happen next session: that you will meet again as a family, that you will see them by themselves and help them with parenting, that you will see the teen individually and in general terms explain why. You track the process and make sure that both are comfortable with this arrangement.

The Need for Confidentiality Is Heightened

The worlds of teens and parents are much more separate than that of younger children and parents. Teens are sensitive to privacy and so confidentiality is heightened; any perceived violation will shatter trust.

You need to assure teens that your conversations with them are confidential, and also describe the limits of that confidentiality—potential danger to self or others—as soon as possible, ideally in the first session. It is usually in those gray zones—the teen who is smoking a lot of marijuana or cutting, for example—where you need to use your clinical judgment and either focus on the problem under the problem in family therapy (depression, anxiety), or make the decision to shift the focus to individual therapy for the teen with you or someone else. This determination becomes part of your negotiation with the teen. You need to be sensitive to these boundaries if you are to be effective.

What the adolescents bring to first sessions of family therapy is what we would expect of their developmental stage as half child–half adult: at times making the process seem more like that of a younger child and parent, and other times having more in common with that of a couple. Your challenge is to be aware of these age differences when working with younger children and teens, while continuing to maintain your leadership role.

First Session Process with Families

Let's now walk through the process of the first session with families using the families of Chris and Amy as models. As in Chapter 3, we'll break the session down into its components with discussion of decision points along the way.

Preparing Ahead

Chris and you exchange voice messages and set up an appointment, and though he initially said that the older brother, Nat, 11 years old, would be coming as well, Chris calls to say that Nat won't be able to make it because of an after-school conflict. He asks if that is okay or do they need to reschedule?

If you are a staunch believer in total family therapy for the first session or suspect Nat may play a major role in the family's particular dynamic, you may reschedule. You decide that this isn't important enough right now to change the appointment, and if you feel you need to touch base with Nat, you can discuss this with the parents at this first session. The larger question circles around your thoughts about Joel: The fidgetiness at school is obviously one possible symptom of ADHD, but, as mentioned earlier, this can also come from changes in the family, some trauma, or Joel simply being bored by too-easy school work. Since you didn't get a chance to ask Chris if there is any history of ADHD in the family or any recent family changes, you'll have to wait and see. You're wondering how Joel will behave in the session, how active he might become, and you check to see if the playroom is available during that hour in case you want to pull Joel off to see him by himself. The room is not available, so you'll have to see what evolves in the session.

Amy, on the other hand, is able to have a brief conversation with you on the phone. In addition to mentioning her concerns about Chloe—the attitude, drop in grades, questions about the boyfriend—Amy says that Chloe is refusing to come in and see you. You coach Amy on asking Chloe to come this one time, telling Chloe that she doesn't need to talk, but just listen so that Amy has a safe place to get some things off her chest. You tell Amy that it is your job to see if Chloe can speak up and be willing to come back. You also say to Amy that she can tell Chloe that she is welcome to call you before the session if she has any questions or just to hear the sound of your voice. Amy sounds relieved.

This one-session no-need-to-talk approach generally works well for resistant teens (or partners in couple relationships). Often they're anxious about what might unfold: the sense of being put on the spot, somehow hooked into becoming the patient and getting stuck in therapy for an indefinite period, or being attacked by the parent. Your job is to make the session safe all around, and the one-session no-need-to-talk pass usually is enough to reduce these fears. And as you said to Amy, the responsibility becomes yours to help the resistant family member open up and possibly return. If Chloe decides not to come, you'll need to meet with Amy, and gather more information to decide on Plan B: Find other ways of drawing

Chloe in, or working with Amy to change the conversation and dynamics between them and in the home.

But you're also brainstorming, as with Joel, what might be going on in this family. Sudden changes in an adolescent's behavior can come from a myriad of sources in addition to family changes: problems with peers or boyfriends, long-standing depression and self-esteem issues, drug use, as well as poor communication and lack of or overstructuring in the home. Again, you'll have to wait and see what evolves.

Part 1a: The Opening

Chris, Kim, and Joel come for the first session. Both Chris and Kim appear to be in their 30s; Joel is a red-headed, solidly-built child who seems large for his age. Chris takes the lead coming into your office, Kim and Joel behind. Chris and Kim sit together on the couch and Joel immediately walks over to your bookcase and scans the books, pulling some of them out. Chris speaks up in a stern voice and tells Joel to sit down in the chair to the side of them. He does, but then fidgets—kicking his legs, wiggling. He asks if he can play his Game Boy, and Kim, in a softer voice, says that he needs to sit still right now for a few minutes.

You ask Joel if he knows where he is—often young children have no idea; they are just told that they are going to the doctor's—and they sometimes worry that you are like their family physician who is going to examine them or, worse yet, give them an injection. Joel shakes his head no, and you quietly say that you are not like a doctor he goes to when he is sick, but a worry doctor who helps children with problems they may be having at home and school. Joel doesn't say anything back, but continues to shake is leg and scan the room.

You ask the parents if they looked at your website. Chris

says he has, Kim says that she meant to but didn't have a chance. You quickly give her a summary of your background, ask them both how long they have been married—12 years—if they have any other children besides Nat—they don't—whether this is a first marriage for each of them—it is—what they do for jobs, and whether they have been in family therapy before—they haven't. In order to include him in the conversation right away, you ask Joel about his brother and why he didn't come, and he says he doesn't know. You ask him what school he goes to—he tells you—and his teacher's name. You also ask who his best friend is—he says Harry—and then Kim pipes up and says to Joel, "What about Morgan? He's a good friend too, isn't he?"—and Joel doesn't answer.

You notice that Chris took the lead in answering several of the questions, and you are relieved that Kim, though seemingly quieter, is speaking up. She's not shy or closed off—a good sign.

Like Joel, Chloe comes in trailing her mother. Amy is in her 40s and looks bedraggled and slumped over. Chloe, in contrast, stands up straight, is wearing makeup, and plops herself in the chair to the side of her mother, who is on the couch. You thank Chloe for coming, and she shrugs. You ask her if she and her mother had talked about coming, and she says, a bit. You ask her if she has been in counseling before, and she says no, not really, but she has talked to the guidance counselor at school a couple times in the past month. How come, you ask, and she says it was about her grades and changing some classes at the beginning of the year.

Again, you give them both a brief summary of your background. You ask who else is in their family, and Amy mentions Roger. "Who's Roger?" you ask. Chloe speaks up and says to her mother in a stern voice that no, Roger is not in their family anymore. "I'm sorry," you say, "I'm confused." In a quiet voice Amy says that Roger was Chloe's stepfather, but he died 3 months ago in a car accident. You can tell Amy is pushing back tears. Chloe looks annoyed and turns away. You say you are so sorry to hear that, and deliberately choose to not focus on Amy's emotion so early the session; you have time, and you don't want to move too quickly, especially after noticing Chloe's reaction. As with Kim and Joel, you're relieved that Chloe, in spite of her anticipated reluctance, is speaking up.

Part 1b: Client Story
"How can I help?" you ask.

"Joel, sit still!" Chris yells at Joel. Joel has gotten up again to look at books, but he sits back down.

"I guess, what we're struggling with," says Kim, in her quiet voice, "is this type of behavior." She reaches over to pat Joel on the leg.

Chris goes on to explain how Joel has been getting in trouble at school for not staying in his seat, for not paying attention in class. At home he does much of the same: He has trouble doing his homework, loses his assignments, or says that he finished them at school, when he hasn't. He was at a birthday party last weekend and grabbed the largest piece of the cake, rather than waiting for the parent to hand out pieces to the children.

You ask Joel about school. Does he have a hard time sometimes?—sometimes. Does he get bored?—sometimes. What does he like to do most? Play outside with his friends or play videogames. Any favorite video games?—he names a couple you haven't heard of.

You're trying to engage him, but you can see that he is

having trouble both focusing and staying still. Again, although Chris seems to be the parent who is both more easily frustrated and sterner, you're relieved that Kim spoke up and that their worries are shared.

You ask Amy and Chloe how you can help, and Amy begins reciting all the things she mentioned on the phone: that Chloe has an negative attitude and is irritable all the time, that she (Amy) doesn't know how to talk to her, that her grades are slipping, that she (Amy) is worried about the boyfriend.

"You've heard this before?" you ask Chloe.

"All the time."

"Your mom is worried about you. Are you worried about you? Your grades, your mood?"

"No, I'm worried about her."

"What do you mean?"

"All she does," Chloe says, gesturing toward her mother, "is mope about the house or stay in bed."

"What worries you about that?"

"She doesn't *do* anything. She's depressed. I hate it." As she says this, her voice softens.

"Did you know that Chloe is worried about you?" you ask Amy.

"No, I guess not, not really. She's right, I haven't been doing well these past few months."

"Can you tell me about Roger?"

Amy tears up again.

"This is what I'm talking about," says Chloe, her voice becoming annoyed again.

Let's pause here. Do you have any concerns or impressions about either case? Time-wise you're doing okay—only about 15 or 20 minutes have passed. There's time for further assessment. Joel is obviously struggling, which you note as he replicates his behavioral problem at school here in your office. If you had the playroom you would carve out a few minutes to see how he is one on one, especially since he seems more or less comfortable with you. But it's not an option, so you'll have to wait. You decide that it would be a better use of time to see if Joel and the parents are comfortable with his staying in the supervised waiting area next door, where he can play with his Game Boy, while you gather more information from the parents. You can see Joel individually next time.

Now to Amy and Chloe: You do need to help them talk about Roger. His death has understandably been a huge loss and change for this family and Amy is clearly depressed and grieving. Chloe probably is no doubt grieving as well, but in contrast to Amy's sadness, Chloe is more irritable. That fact that she was able to say that she is worried about Amy is good, in that she can say it and that it reflects a strong emotional connection to her mom. You worry, however, that being the only child, she may be feeling a pull to step up and take care of Mom, to hold her grief in check and appear strong because Mom clearly is not so. With a change in the family structure, Chloe may be testing the limits, as well as beginning to act up to help pull Amy out of her depression. Finally, Chloe may be gravitating toward the boyfriend for support or some emotional replacement for Roger.

All this is speculation, of course, but still requires further exploration. Right now your goal is to change the emotional climate, move Chloe out of her annoyed stance, deepen the conversation between mother and daughter, and find out what Chloe wants in order to give her a reason to come back.

Part 2: Assessment

You ask Chris and Kim if it would be okay with them if Joel went out to the waiting area and entertained himself with his Game Boy while the three of you talked. They are fine, and then you ask Joel if he wouldn't mind going to the waiting room next door for a few minutes. Not surprisingly, he seems relieved and hustles out.

Although your initial hunch seems to you to be on target—that Joel has ADHD—you ask the parents what you need to know to rule out other possibilities. So you ask how long these behaviors have been going on; you ask if there is a family history of ADHD, and Chris admits that he was actually diagnosed in middle school and takes low-dose ADHD medication himself. No, there have not been any changes in the family, Nat doesn't show any of the same behaviors, and you run through your checklist of ADHD symptoms. You ask if the school has done any assessment of its own, and it has not. You also ask about how they manage those situations at home when Joel seems to be having a hard time. Throughout, you're watching the clock. You only have a few more minutes before you need to shift toward presenting your plan.

"Well," says Chris, "what do you mean by a *hard time?* I think my tolerance is a bit lower than Kim's, and I'm apt to discipline him more quickly."

"And a bit more bluntly," says Kim. "I feel Chris just snaps at Joel at times. I try to be more patient; I try to explain to Joel how what he is doing isn't appropriate. Chris doesn't do that."

This is okay, you think. They both are speaking up—they are sharing responsibility and seem balanced in power;

both are acknowledging style and emotional differences, but Chris isn't getting defensive and arguing back. You can imagine, however, that they need to be more on the same page for Joel to have the clear and consistent structure that he needs. You wonder if Chris can balance out his disciplinarian stance with some nurturance in order to foster a good relationship with Joel. Finally, you wonder if Nat is a hard act for Joel to follow—all more areas for further exploration.

You ask Chloe about what upsets her about Amy's feeling sad over the loss of Roger.

"I think she needs to move on. It's been 3 months, after all."

"So Roger was your stepdad. Had he been living with you long?"

"Yeah, he was there since I was 6. He was really my dad." Her voice is softening again.

"What do you mean? Where's you're biological dad? Do you see him?"

"No, he left when I was 2. Every couple of years maybe I get a Christmas card, but I haven't seen him since I was maybe 4—right, Mom?"

"Yeah, about then. He stopped by once unexpectedly when he was passing through."

"Anyhow, now he has another family and kids in California."

"So Roger stepped in and became your real dad?"

"Yeah."

"What do you miss about Roger?" you ask softly.

"Well, he and I used to do stuff." Chloe begins to tear up.

"Like what?" *(You ask details to move her more deeply into her emotions.)*

"Like go fishing together. Or he would take me out on his motorcycle. . . ." Tears begin to flow.

You look over at Amy. She too is tearing.

"And what do you miss most, Amy?"

"Just having him around, I guess. Coffee together on Saturday mornings. Walking the dog."

Chloe is crying more deeply now. She seems to be able to stay with her emotions, but you are watching closely to see if she may flare up or bolt out of the room to cut it off. She doesn't.

"Chloe," says Amy, "I'm so sorry that I haven't been there for you these past months. I know you've been suffering, but I haven't known what to do. I know you miss Roger like I do. I'm so sorry this has been so hard on you."

Chloe looks away, but now both are crying. You look down and give them space.

Part 3: Presenting the Treatment Plan and Summary
"Thanks for coming in today," you say to Chris and Kim. "Let me tell you what I'm thinking."

You then go on to say that, based on what they have described, the family history, and what you observed while Joel was in the session, you believe that Joel probably has ADHD. It is genetic, a brain disorder of the executive functioning, and treatment is usually a combination of medication and behavioral management.

"We actually had thought that that is probably what the problem is," says Kim. "Chris takes medication, but I'm not sure how I feel about medication for Joel. He's young."

Kim raises an understandable and common concern or objection about medication that you need to address.

Some children don't need medication, you explain; it depends on how severe their symptoms are and how they can be managed with behavioral interventions. Yes, you say, you are aware that medication raises some biological concerns.

"What I'd like to do, since we didn't have time to do it today," you say, "is meet with Joel individually next week in the playroom to get a better idea of him and his behavior. I can get a better idea of how severe his ADHD might be or even if there are other issues that may be creating his behaviors. If medication might need to be considered, I can then refer you to a child psychiatrist who can evaluate him regarding medication and options, and you can discuss with him any concerns that you may have. How does that sound?"

Both Chris and Kim nod their heads. Chris says that he is fine with that and doesn't have the concern with medication that Kim does, since he knows firsthand how it has helped him. Kim says that she doesn't want to rush into meds.

"I understand," you say, "that's why we can take it slowly. There's also a lot that I can help you both do at home in terms of routines and structure that may help Joel settle more easily and you both to feel less frustrated. I'm also happy to talk with the school. We can consider individual therapy for Joel as well to teach him some regulation skills, and I'd like to meet Nat at some point.

"Again, I'll have a better idea after I see him alone next week. If you're both willing, I'd like to get a release to talk to this teacher at school. Does all this make sense and sound okay? Does this fit with what you were hoping we would do?"

They both strongly agree. Good to go.

Although you had planned on meeting with Joel in the next session anyway, your plan has the added benefit of helping counter Kim's objection. You are taking it slowly, assessing further, helping her to avoid feeling railroaded into considering medication. You are also being sensitive to her possible transference issues—deliberately being a counter to Chris, who tends to march ahead on his own, and you suspect, sometimes overlooks her feelings.

Your plan also addresses what you see as the clinical need to have them work together and create a coordinated structure at home. If they can put this structure in place and both be on the same page, working as a team, Chris's frustration is likely to decrease, which in turn will help Kim feel less annoyed by it and less inclined to compensate for it with Joel.

Amy and Chloe are beginning to calm themselves. You've done a good job of changing the emotional climate in the room. Rather than being emotionally polarized—with Amy sad and Chloe annoyed—they both are able to openly express their grief and perhaps have the beginnings of a conversation that they have been unable to have on their own.

"Chloe," you say quietly, "your mom wanted you to come here together because she is worried about how you've been doing lately—your mood, your grades *(you deliberately skip mentioning the boyfriend for now, since that may stir up a separate can of worms)*. I'm wondering what it is that you want changed the most at home between you both."

She sighs, then shrugs. "I guess I'd like my mom to do better so I don't have to worry about her so much."

"Anything else?"

"I guess I'd like us to be able to do more together. We haven't done that, not just recently but for a long time. We both kinda paired off with Roger, which was great, but she and I haven't done much together for a long time. I'd like to do more."

Clearly Chloe is articulate and mature beyond her years.

"What do you think about that Amy?"

"That would be great, I'd like that."

"What I'm impressed by is how much you both care about each other. You both have suffered a tremendous and sudden loss, and as in most families, usually each person handles her grief differently. Understandably, Amy, you've withdrawn, and you, Chloe, have perhaps gotten more irritable and moody. Does this make sense?"

You're tracking the process. They both nod.

"There's also a hole in the family that instinctively needs to be filled. I'm wondering if you, Chloe, are feeling some pressure to take care of your mom, especially since she seems to be struggling so much. Have you?"

"I guess. I worry about her all the time, but I don't say anything about it because I don't want to get her more upset. I've been trying to help out more around the house, and I worry sometimes about money."

"I didn't know you were worrying about that," says Amy.

"This is easy to happen," you say, "especially in families with an older or only child. I just wonder, Chloe, if worry has been weighing on you and has affected your schoolwork and mood."

"Yeah, I guess so."

"I'd like to help you both find a way of getting through this difficult time together. I'm wondering if it has been hard for both of you to talk together about Roger."

They nod. "That's something you can certainly do on your own, but we can also do that here, if that feels easier. Sharing your feelings like you did today is part of getting through this and staying connected. Underneath it all, I'd guess that you are both probably feeling the same, but have been showing it differently. Does this make sense?"

They both nod. "What I'd like to do is split the session next time, see you both for about a half hour, just so I can get to know you each better as an individual. Is that okay?"

Again, they both agree.

"For homework, I'd like you to try and do what you both said—that is, spend some time together maybe this weekend. Doesn't have to be big and dramatic, but something you might both enjoy. Think about it, talk about it, and give it a try. Okay?"

Again, they nod their heads. They are ready to move forward.

So, what have you accomplished in this first session with these two different families? With Chris and Kim, you have checked out, sufficiently for now, your initial hypothesis that Joel has ADHD. You've allayed Kim's initial objections about medication. You're comfortable that the parents, though they have different communication styles that need fine-tuning, are not showing any red flags for more concerning parenting or marital issues. And you essentially changed the emotional climate through education, and met their expectations. You clearly know what your next steps are and have their support.

Amy and Chloe did wonderfully. Although you were braced for Chloe's possible resistance, it didn't materialize. If it had—with Amy ranting and Chloe shutting down—you would have separated them to connect to Chloe and develop a clear, therapeutic contract. You changed the emotional climate by tracking those softer emotions, in particular those of Chloe. You were fortunate that she was mature, articulate, and sensitive. You realize that you may need to be careful about falling into unintentionally filling Roger's role in the family—where both Amy and Chloe both feel better because they get from you emotionally, in some way, what they used to get from him. This is why you want to focus on helping them stay connected to each other and helping Amy step up into the parenting role so Chloe can step down and be a normal teen. But right now you have helped them bridge the emotional gap between them and can focus on guiding them through this family transition.

This overview of two cases is, of course, just one approach to such family problems. Your own clinical approach will perhaps be different, but the first-session themes and goals remain the same: following the process, watching the clock, and having time to accomplish your goals of building rapport, clarifying expectations, gathering the information you need to confirm or develop your hypothesis and treatment plan, and making sure the clients are all onboard. Again, what is more challenging here, as it was with couples, is dealing with not just one individual, but several. This multiplicity translates into tracking the process tightly, demonstrating greater leadership, and formulating a treatment plan that addresses the concerns of everyone in the room.

CHAPTER 7

Beyond the First Session

YOU'VE ACCOMPLISHED THAT all-important first session and laid down a solid foundation on which to build. Your next challenge approaches: that of keeping the momentum going so you and the client can successfully move into the thick of treatment.

In this chapter we'll talk about exactly that—map out some of the common clinical tasks of the second and third sessions, as well as note the possible challenges that can arise. The aim here, as with the first session, is to help you become familiar with the landscape so you can anticipate and prepare for what may come next. By way of summary, we'll also talk about the four essential elements on which you need to focus to keep the momentum going. Finally, we'll conclude this chapter by considering ways you can incorporate some of the clinical elements of the first session into your own therapeutic style.

Second Session Goals and Challenges

Ideally, each session should flow from the last with all moving toward your and your clients' ultimate goals. Second sessions are no different. They are about next steps but also about bridges and corrections to what went on before. Here are common foci of second sessions:

Do Relationship Repair

Maybe you had a tinge of worry after your session with Ben and Sera, the couple we discussed in Chapter 5, that you left Ben feeling a bit ganged up on, but the worry wasn't strong enough to motivate you to call. At the start of the second session, however, you decide to speak up: "Ben, in thinking about the last session, I began to wonder if you felt that Sera and I were ganging up on you and giving you a hard time." And then you see what Ben says next—"Yes, a bit but that's okay"; "Yes, a lot, and it really bothered me"; "No, not at all."

For the "a bit" and "a lot" you want to zero in—see what upset him the most, explain your intentions, be sensitive to his reactions, and help him feel safe. Sometimes the seemingly solid "No" is actually not that solid, but the client is not comfortable enough yet to speak up; you accept the answer, but mentally note it and continue to track the process. For now you've done what you can by approaching the topic and letting the client know that how he feels and what bothers him in a session are always important to discuss and should not be dismissed.

Assessing the state of the therapeutic relationship and making repairs along the way are essential for preventing resistance. Although the bulk of this work will occur in those first opening sessions, it is something that you want to stay aware of throughout the treatment process. It's part and parcel of sensitivity, problem solving, and modeling how to approach anxiety and how to create good relationships.

Check on Homework

As mentioned in Chapter 2, there is value in assigning homework at the end of the first session. Homework can offer a source of continuing assessment—asking Marc, for example, to notice what he is thinking when he feels depressed, or asking Melinda to look for any triggers that set off a binge episode during the week. It also builds on the energy and changed emotional climate of the first session, creating momentum. And finally, it is a way of letting you know about the therapeutic relationship. If Marc and Melinda don't bother with their assignments, the next question is *why*: Were the assignments too unclear or overwhelming? Did they not see the value because you failed to connect the assignments to their primary concerns? Or is there a problem in the therapeutic relationship—are they ambivalent about you or your approach and so aren't motivated to do what you asked?

Of course, you'll only know by asking, and that's what you do in the second session: uncover any problems under the problem of not doing homework. If you forget or brush it aside, it gives the message to clients that the homework isn't really important and is, at best, an optional supplement to treatment.

Continue Your Assessment

In the last chapter, you said to Joel's parents that you wanted to spend the second session seeing him by himself in a play therapy setting. This is needed because you weren't able to get a solid impression of him in the family session, and because you want to see how he acts differently in a one-on-one situation. You are gathering the additional information you need to confirm your diagnosis.

Similarly, many therapists separate couples or members of a family—as you proposed to do to Amy and Chloe in the last chapter—in the second session, essentially splitting the time, to help mentally separate the individuals from the relationship dynamics. This one-on-one time not only provides a way of repairing relationships—for example, seeing Ben by himself in the second session to make certain that he didn't feel ganged up on—but also allows you to further explore any individual issues—one partner's one-sentence statement in the first session about "some childhood trauma," the extent of a family member's addiction, the level of someone's depression—and to explore sensitive topics that a partner or family member may withhold talking about with others—Chloe, for example, talking more openly about her boyfriend without her mother in the room.

Other clinicians may continue assessment by doing some type of testing—a simple depression or addiction scale, or a more formal tool such as an MMPI (Minnesota Muliphasic Personality Inventory). Whatever assessment you plan on doing, it should come as no surprise to the client; ideally, you've discussed this further assessment plan at the end of the first session and have already managed any objections.

Whatever your assessment plans, you need to be flexible. So, although you planned on seeing Ben and Sera separately, they come in saying that they really need to talk about the argument they had on Saturday night; you let them talk about Saturday night. You planned to do testing, but your client is jet-lagged and is struggling to stay focused and alert. You push your plans to the back burner and let your client set the agenda.

Teach Skills

Teaching specific skills in the second session is an excellent way of continuing the momentum. You could, for example, spend the second session teaching Tom (whom we met in Chapter 4, and who was struggling with anxiety) several anxiety management techniques such as deep breathing, meditation, mindfulness, Emotional Freedom Technique, and so on. Not only does teaching these skills address his presenting problems quickly, the practicing of the techniques during the week is valuable homework that lets you know what is and is not effective with Tom and where and how he may get stuck.

Similarly, you could role-play with a client talking with her supervisor about her schedule, map out with a violent couple a first-aid plan to keep discussions from escalating, or help parents create a reward chart that they can use with their children. Again, you plan, but are flexible. If the client is still in crisis and comes in with a specific agenda, you'll need to try and incorporate your skill training into his or her current needs, or simply postpone it until the client is more settled.

Follow up with no-shows. This is the biggest challenge of the second session: that clients don't come back. They either call and provide some reasonable excuse why they can't come in and how they will give you a call when they know their schedule, or they simply don't show.

Ideally, these situations should be rare if you've done a good job building a relationship and handling objections in the first session, but sometimes it happens. They really do have an unexpected change in their weekly schedule, realize that they really can't afford the copayments, or they were actually shopping around and settled on a different therapist who was a better fit, suddenly and unexpectedly things improved—a

good work evaluation, a change of heart from their partner—
or they simply got cold feet in spite of your efforts.

Whatever the possible reason, your next step, as we mentioned in Chapter 4, is to call them and let them know you've
received their message, see if they want to reschedule, and
discuss their reservations and concerns to try and solve the
problem—setting an appointment in 2 months after they
get back from their business project in China, working with
them on a extended payment plan, asking gently why they've
changed their mind about therapy. And if they don't want
to engage and simply need to stop for whatever reason, you
let them know they are welcome to come back at any time.
And if they don't respond, follow up with the same message—
through voicemail or a note, thank them for coming in and let
them know they are welcome to come back at any point.

It's important to document all of the above for potential
ethical and liability issues. You don't want to be in a position
where a client doesn't show up for some reason; in his mind
he intends to return, but because you didn't reach out to him,
he assumed that you were cutting him off for the no-show.
If he should fall into crisis or worst-case scenario, commit
suicide, the family could accuse you of abandonment. After
making a couple of attempts at contact, some clinicians, as
mentioned earlier, send a certified letter stating that they are
assuming that because there has been no contact, the client
has decided to discontinue services and that they are closing
the case. Your protection is to reach out and document that
you did so.

Third Session Goals and Challenges

In the third session you may continue many of the tasks of the second session—still checking on homework, still seeing various family members or individual partners, teaching skills, continuing assessment—but generally you should be rounding the corner into the middle stages of treatment. It is here, however, where you may discover some new variations in the clinical landscape.

Third Session Drop-Out

Yes, clients may drop out after the first session for practical reasons or questions about style and fit, but it is often in the third or fourth session that clients discontinue for other reasons. Here are some of the common sources:

The Crisis Is Over. Tom practices your anxiety-reducing techniques, is feeling more confident and decides he is good to go. Ben and Sera go off for an extended weekend trip, don't argue and actually have a great time, and decide they are cured. Chloe breaks up with her boyfriend, is hanging around the house more, and Amy is no longer so worried and stops coming.

Although you think there is more work to do to firmly put the problem to rest, you've helped them take enough of the edge off the problem and their worry to inspire them to move on. Once again you call and welcome them to come back anytime.

Anxiety Sets in. With the settling of the crisis or the telling of the story, the client not only feels better by getting things off her chest, but she also feels anxious. Now that the overwhelming emotional fog has lifted, she is more present in the room and worries what you are really thinking about all that she has said; or she doesn't know what to talk about in the third session now that the story is out and over, and is worried about "going deeper."

This is where you want to anticipate and articulate, perhaps in the second session when you sense the client is winding down, what the landscape may look like in the next session. If she's a no-show for the third session, call and say what you think she may be thinking: that she is nervous, perhaps, now that the crisis has settled, and may not be sure what to focus on, that this is normal, and you'd like to help her with this.

Transference Issues Come to the Fore. You've done your best to uncover transference cues all along, but with the settling of the crisis and lifting of the emotional fog, Amy realizes that she really does have a difficult time talking intimately with men and needs to see a female therapist; or Tom liked the idea of learning skills, but now feels that your personalities don't match, and his doubts and the less-than-comfortable feeling he has sitting with you in the session cause him to bolt. Reach out, say what you think, see if you can help allay fears, but then let go and respect their decision.

Sabotage by Family Members. A not-uncommon scenario is one in which Sera, for example, comes in by herself for the first session to talk about her problems with Ben. She goes home, tells Ben that she saw you about their relationship and that you suggested that they come back together as a couple. Ben is anxious about the whole notion of therapy, or now feels that you've bonded with Sera and he is already in the emotional doghouse. In either case, he promises Sera that he will change, be kinder and gentler, and he is. Sera, not wanting to risk shaking up a good thing, drops out.

If there's not a Ben, there may be a grandmother who

lambastes therapy and talking to strangers about private business; or Chloe's boyfriend convinces her that therapy is just for weirdoes, that the problems are all with her mother, and Amy falls back into her depression. Again, you do what you can—reach out, call Amy and Chloe and see if either one of them is willing to come in, and say what you think they may be thinking. You say the door is always open.

Mandated Clients. Harry is ordered to therapy for anger management, comes twice, then calls and says that he needs to work overtime for the next 2 months. He's talked to his attorney about it, who said that since he did come in twice and has a legitimate reason to not attend sessions, the judge will probably not sanction him. Harry drops out.

Harry didn't want to come to begin with, but he's done enough to get the court off his back. You reach out, document it, then let him go.

The theme here is that you can't control clients and there is a host of issues that can lead to their withdrawal. The best you can do is anticipate, say what you think to get issues on the table, try and resolve the problem under the problem, and then welcome them back so that guilt doesn't prevent their possible return in the future.

Couples and Families Seem to Get Worse. This is a different dynamic and hopefully they don't drop out. You may be moving along through the first two sessions, feeling confident that everyone is onboard, and positive changes, albeit small, are happening, but then they come in the third or fourth session and everything is in shambles. Ben and Sera were doing great, but over the weekend they again had a blowup that was worse than any in the past. Amy and Chloe were doing well, but Amy exploded in the last session, causing Chloe to stomp out of the room.

This seeming deterioration is rattling to new or less experienced therapists. More experienced folks know to take this turn of events in stride, that it's probably not a sign of mistakes on their part, a missing of something vitally important in the beginning, but more a reflection of the couple or family's increased sense of comfort and safety. Ben and Sera actually may have had similar blowups in the weeks before, but are now comfortable processing them with you and each other. Amy's been ready to explode for a long time, but now with her feeling more comfortable and supported by you, is able to express what she has been holding back. You don't panic or beat yourself up; you help the couple or family put out the emotional fire in the room.

You Uncover Serious Individual Problems. Uncovering serious individual problems is a variation of the preceding section. Chloe tells you in the third session that she has been cutting; Tom says that he is actually worried about how much he drinks; Sera mentions sexual abuse from her childhood that she has never spoken to anyone about. Again, these are all signs that you are doing a good job and that there is safety and trust in the therapeutic relationship.

You task is to decide what to do with this new information. If you are working with a family or couple, the question is whether you feel the individual needs individual work to deal with these issues. As mentioned in Chapter 5, you would most likely want to suggest to Tom that he get a substance abuse evaluation. The question for Chloe may be whether her cutting is recent and tied to the grief and tension in the home: Will a change in the home climate relieve the cutting, or has the cutting, in fact, been a long-standing means of coping for her? Similarly, you want to determine whether and how much

Sera's childhood abuse may or may not severely impact the marital relationship.

These are all clinical judgment calls, issues of exploration, style, and need for discussion. You want to talk with Tom, Chloe, and Sera further, form your own clinical impressions, and discuss clinical options with them. If, for example, you decide to shift toward providing individual therapy for Chloe or Sera, you need to anticipate and eventually determine how much the family or couple therapy is unbalanced.

You may, for example, use an individual session to help Chloe develop a first-aid plan for herself to apply when she feels the urge to cut; see how well the plan works, and see how the family therapy relieves the stress that ignites the cutting. If, after a few weeks there is no change in her behavior, you may recommend to Chloe that she consider individual therapy to provide more support, and that you will continue to see her and Amy together to continue to work on family issues.

Similarly, you and Sera may decide that she needs some intensive work to process the early abuse, that you are willing to take it on, and that couple therapy for now is on hold. At some point down the road, when the trauma is no longer on the front burner, you can reevaluate the need for couple therapy with you or someone else.

Marital Issues Come to the Fore. It's not uncommon for parents to present with family/child issues, and by the third or fourth session, either to drop the issues all together and begin to talk about underlying marital issues; or uncover them through your assessment and realize that these issues are, in fact, what are driving the children's problems. And so with their agreement, you shift focus.

But sometimes, as with Chloe and Amy, you need to provide a two-pronged treatment. You may help the parents with the marital issues and see one of the children in play therapy to help with anxiety. Or depending on your skill, schedule, and comfort, you may refer the parents for couple counseling with someone else and you stay with the child, or vice versa.

The thread running through all these possible shifts in the third session is that of accumulation: increased safety, increased transference issues, increased competency and reduction of crisis, increased complexity, and increased unraveling of underlying issues. Some of these you expect, but some may take you by surprise. Again, you anticipate as best you can, but because the map isn't the terrain, you need not criticize yourself for some failing, only address these twists and turns as they arise. This is what makes for the improvisational quality of therapy.

Three Essential Elements for Maintaining Momentum

Just as there are essential goals that you need to cover in the first session to make it successful, there are three essential elements that you need to keep on the front burner throughout the treatment process in order to maintain momentum and reach your destination.

1. Start Treatment Right Away

There is the old adage that termination starts in the first session. What this means is that not only are you looking ahead proactively toward what needs to be accomplished, but also that treatment and assessment actually go hand in hand.

Said another way, you don't want to do assessment for a huge length of time before starting treatment, especially in a therapy world where the average length of therapy is five to eight sessions.

So, if you want to build on momentum, you really can't afford to simply assess for weeks on end. This is like the worried patient who fears he has cancer, spends months seeing specialists, and gets tests with no definitive feedback. Yes, assessment can double as treatment, such as when you assign homework, but you want to make clear to the client that you are both, in fact, on the path of treatment and change.

We're back to matching expectations and staying in lockstep. You see clients as soon as possible because their motivation and energy are the highest at the moment they call you. You offer your treatment plan in the first session because they want to leave with something, and you leave them with a vision that they've come to the right place and the right person and that change is going to happen. And you start treatment in some form to keep them from losing energy and focus and becoming discouraged and frustrated.

2. Track and Update Expectations And Goals

Tracking the process and staying in lockstep are continual processes that are essential to overall effective treatment. Once treatment is underway, you want to check in periodically—say, every four or five sessions—to view the larger landscape: Is the relationship still strong? Are you and the client focused on the same goal, in step with the overall approach and process? You ask and see what the client says next. If you notice a shift—the client has canceled appointments lately or seems to have little to say in the session or doesn't have a clear agenda—

you raise your concerns. Maybe you've reached an impasse, maybe the client is distracted or burned out by therapy or outside concerns; you want to know.

The bigger danger, however, isn't that the client is somehow dissatisfied, but that both of you have fallen into a particular comfort zone. Here we're talking about possible dependency, an ethical issue, where there is a good relationship but little real change. Both you and client are going on autopilot, have fallen into a rut, which might be good or bad but a rut nonetheless.

There are usually two sources of this condition. One is that therapy actually isn't working; you don't have the skill or approach to fix the client's problem, but can't fully admit it to yourself. You falsely believe that you both just need to do more of what you're already doing, that something will "click" at some point and the client will make gains, that the losses are temporary. The client may be unhappy but either has not been in therapy before, doesn't know what to expect, and is trusting you to lead the way; or is afraid to speak up and voice his or her concerns, often replicating the presenting problem.

But the other source of dependency is more subtle and powerful. It is that situation where the relationship itself overrides the momentum of treatment. The therapist and client are now like an old married couple in their comfort zones of intimacy and safety; they both even look forward to seeing the other. You meet every Tuesday at 2 P.M. because you meet every Tuesday at 2 P.M. Yes, sometimes this predictability is, in fact, the treatment. The fact that Frank checks in with his therapist every week and doesn't talk about much is actually fine because it is the checking in, connection, and accountability that keep Frank from going off the rails; if he didn't see his therapist weekly, he would go off his meds or fall back into his addiction and stop coming. This context, however, is very different from those situations where the spoken goal is something else, and the unspoken goal is that the therapist and client collude to not risk disrupting the relationship even though the treatment isn't working.

The antidote to this stalemate is supervision or colleague feedback of some kind, but more importantly, self-awareness, self-honesty, and planned and periodic evaluation of goals and process with the client. This component of evaluation is part and parcel of customer satisfaction and clinical leadership.

3. Continue to Track and Explore Transference Issues

The third element that can kill momentum is the igniting of old emotional wounds. Yes, like it or not, you will probably trigger some strong emotional baggage at some point and you'll need to repair—this is part of most therapy—but having a clear map of "how to respond" should be part of your own treatment plan.

Ideally, you want to be able to know what *not* to do with a particular client as quickly as possible—again, knowing how to be the specific ideal parent, knowing how to avoid triggering these strong and distorted emotional reactions. The danger, most especially for less experienced clinicians, is that they think they've nailed down the major concerns, and then they stop looking for the subtleties and variations as treatment progresses.

You may know, for example, that you need to be the "not-Amy" with Chloe—you need to be supportive, engaged, noncritical—if you are to gain rapport with her—but you don't know yet how to be the not-boyfriend or not-father and don't pay it enough attention. Chloe may feel that you are dismissing her at some point, the way her father did or her boyfriend does, and she drops out. Or worse, she doesn't drop out, but says nothing and continues to feel hurt, taking what she gets. Rather than fixing the problem, you've inadvertently managed only to *replicate* it. As with dependency, the antidote is an outside perspective from a supervisor or colleague, as well as sensitivity to the process and the raising of possible issues with clients as quickly as possible.

What each of these tasks has in common is the focus on process. The content will always change, the conditions in the client's larger world are always variable, but your focus remains the same: namely, on what is unfolding then and there in the room in each and every session.

Incorporating Skills into Your Style

One of the goals of this book has been to challenge your thinking and awareness of your own first sessions. If some of the concepts and skills that we have discussed intrigued you and you would like to find ways of incorporating them into your everyday practice, here are some tips for getting starting:

See Clients Quickly

Most likely you instinctively do this, but sometimes it is easy to underestimate the impact of a crisis or the need to capitalize on a client's motivation. Here you may want to look at your own calendar and caseload. Would it be helpful, for example, for you to leave some appointment slots free in the week for new clients or those in crisis? If you are feeling overloaded in terms of caseload, leaving no availability or long waiting lists, do you need to evaluate the status of some clients, and rather than going on autopilot, discuss termination with an ever-present open-door return policy? Does your clinical model allow for seeing clients in the short term, just to do crisis relief work for, say, one to three sessions, and stating that option at the initial contact? Do you need to be more flexible with your schedule, leaving time for early, before-work appointments a couple of times a week, knowing you can probably offset it with bigger breaks on certain days in the midafternoon?

The point is to be both reflective and proactive in order to make a quick response a priority.

Structure the Session

The overall first-session model presented in Chapter 3 can hopefully help you frame your first sessions. If this idea of choreographing your first sessions is new, you'll need to both plan first sessions with watching the clock in mind, but also deliberately plan to incorporate this framework into some of your sessions.

There are two ways to initiate incorporating this skill. One is to try this with several new clients—intentionally following the framework from start to finish, and asking for feedback along the way. This will help you fine-tune your skills and increase your confidence. The other is to plan to integrate portions of the approach in steps. You may, for example, try sticking to a 20-minute assessment, or a shorter version of your opening for one new client, or try changing how you handle initial contacts, even if you don't yet change other aspects of your approach. Take smaller steps, see how it goes, and fine-tune.

Creating Treatment Maps

As mentioned in Chapter 1, the value of having treatment maps mentally online is to maximize your time in the first session and provide a general outline of next steps for the new client. If you're experienced, you probably have many of these already in place. The question, then, is whether your map is specific enough so that you can outline it for the client in the first session. If you find, for example, that there are gaps—that you need to be able to present more details so clients can leave the first session with a clear sense of what will happen next and what to expect over the course of treatment—take the time to translate concepts into specific behaviors in and out of the session. And if you lack clear maps for certain problems, make time to research models that are compatible with your orientation and style, or talk with a colleague who is particularly good at working with such clients with such problems.

Tracking the Process

This is another skill that, if you are experienced, you no doubt instinctively employ. But if you are less experienced and easily get caught up in content, or follow a clinical model that heavily relies on information and content, you'll want to increase your sensitivity to process. The question to ask yourself in the session is, What is going on in the room right now? Focus on the emotions, the nonverbal behaviors, the emotional connection between you and the client or clients, rather than the story. You may want to periodically practice pausing the content to ask what the client is feeling or to note facial reactions, and so on.

You can also practice such skills in less stressful situations outside the office. When you are having lunch with a friend, shift from the story to the process—"You're rolling your eyes, what's up?"; or with your partner during an end-of-the-day catch-up—"You're quiet, what are you thinking?" Again, it's about skill and shifting your awareness, which is learnable.

And if it's about confrontation—you do well in notic-

ing the process but are anxious about commenting on it—
then this, too, is about practice. Notice the people and places
where this becomes difficult—aggressive men, older women—
and experiment with approaching your anxiety. Yes, you can
say to your friend that he is rolling his eyes, but may hesitate to say the same more diplomatically to your supervisor.
The key is to try and do so, if not in the moment, even later.
The goal is building up your self-confidence by going against
your grain and finding out that, in spite of what your anxious
mind may say, it turns out all right.

Changing the Emotional Climate

We discussed a number of ways to change the emotional climate in Chapter 1. The issue with this skill is partly technique but mostly having a clear intention. The starting point
is setting this as a goal and then looking for opportunities to
act on it.

Looking for soft emotions and using education are the easiest to begin practicing. Anna tears up and you comment on
it. Sam talks about being pissed off and you ask what he's
worried about. You can look for these moments in the session,
and you can practice in conversations with friends and family outside a session. Education tracks along clinical models.
If you have a good model for depression, say, think about a
short educational speech you can give to clients to help them
understand your thinking about depression and its treatment.

Preview and Initial Contacts

How does your voicemail message sound? Ask some colleagues
listen to it and give you feedback. Do you have a website? Can
you develop one? If you have one, does it convey what you
want potential clients to know about you and your approach?

Look at other clinicians' websites and discern what you most like and don't like about them. Have friends give you critical feedback about yours. Listen to new clients' comments when you ask them in the first session whether they looked at your website.

Do you use handout materials for practice guidelines and essential information or as educational material—tips for handling anxiety, guidelines for couple communication, four steps toward anger management, and so on? Would such handouts be helpful, save time, and give clients a better sense of your approach and treatment model?

Do you leave enough time for those initial phone contacts? Are you able to call people back quickly? As suggested above, you might need to adjust your schedule—leave a block of time midday to check messages and return calls, or at least call and let people know that you received their messages and will call again when you have more time to discuss their questions and concerns with them.

There may be other concepts or techniques that have piqued your interest. Again the key is intention, planning ways to both experiment with the concept or skill, and deliberately finding specific ways to gradually incorporate it into your current style and practice. There's a learning curve, so you may feel uncomfortable and rushed at first, but it will all get easier with practice. It's not about changing you and your practice, only enhancing it by building on your strengths.

The Art of the First Session

We've reached the end of this book, a book about beginnings. Like all beginnings in our larger lives, those in therapy are layered with anticipation, anxiety, and awkwardness on both sides. Although therapy is your home, it is not yet the client's. You're the host, the one responsible for welcoming the client in and helping him or her feel comfortable in the therapy world.

The goal of this book has been to help you be that host, quell whatever anxiety you may have by providing a structure for the beginning process, to give it form. Hopefully this structure doesn't restrain you, but instead frees you to be more open and honest, allowing you to show the client what you do and can offer him or her.

By walking through this beginning landscape together, hopefully you have become more aware of the nuances of your own style, your clinical approach to people and problems that is uniquely yours. There is an art to the first session because there is an art to doing therapy. You are the artist, the creator of your own creation that is your therapy style. As you lead the way in building a relationship and new world with each new client, you are also demonstrating to clients how they too can become creators of their own lives.

Isn't this, after all, what therapy is ultimately about?

References

Cain, S. (2012). *Quiet: The power of introverts in a world that can't stop talking*. New York, NY: Crown.

Clifford, C. (2013). *Selling the invisible: Four keys to selling services*. Available online at http://www.youtube.com/watch?v=4HdA924aqbM

Cooper, G. (2011). New perspectives on termination. *Psychotherapy Networker, 35*(5), 10–11.

Doherty, W. (2013). *Take back your marriage*. New York, NY: Guilford Press.

Garfield, S. (2013). Research on client variables in psychotherapy. In S. Garfield & A. Bergin (Eds.), *Handbook of psychotherapy and behavior change* (3rd ed., pp. 213–256). New York, NY: Wiley.

Gottman, I. (2000). *The seven principles for making marriage work: A practical guide from the country's foremost relationship expert*. New York, NY: Harmony.

Hendrix, H. (2007). *Getting the love you want: A guide for couples*. New York, NY: Henry Holt.

Phillips, E. (1985). *Psychotherapy revised: New frontiers in research and practice*. Hillsdale, NJ: Erlbaum.

Pink, D. (2012). *To sell is human: The surprising truth about moving others*. New York, NY: Riverhead Books.

Rehman, S. U. (2005). What to wear today?: Effect of doctor's attire on the trust and confidence of patients. *American Journal of Medicine, 118,* 1279–1286.

Taibbi, R. (2007). *Doing family therapy: Craft and creativity in clinical practice* (2nd ed.). New York, NY: Guilford Press.

Therapy Tribe. *Therapist Marketing Tips: How to Effectively Market Your Practice Online.* Available at http://www.therapytribe.com.

Tracy, B. (2010). *How to improve sales.* Available at http://www.focalpointcoaching.com.

Index